Thomas Hardy's

Tess of the D'Urbervilles

Text by
Charles Grimes
(M.A., Villanova University)
Department of English
Pace University
New York, New York

Illustrations by
Jerilyn Harney-Baker

Research & Education Association

MAXnotes® for
TESS OF THE D'URBERVILLES

Printed in the United States of America

Library of Congress Catalog Card Number 96-67442

International Standard Book Number 0-87891-051-4

MAXnotes® is a registered trademark of
Research & Education Association, Piscataway, New Jersey 08854

What **MAXnotes®** Will Do for You

This book is intended to help you absorb the essential contents and features of Thomas Hardy's *Tess of the D'Urbervilles* and to help you gain a thorough understanding of the work. The book has been designed to do this more quickly and effectively than any other study guide.

For best results, this **MAXnotes** book should be used as a companion to the actual work, not instead of it. The interaction between the two will greatly benefit you.

To help you in your studies, this book presents the most up-to-date interpretations of every section of the actual work, followed by questions and fully explained answers that will enable you to analyze the material critically. The questions also will help you to test your understanding of the work and will prepare you for discussions and exams.

Meaningful illustrations are included to further enhance your understanding and enjoyment of the literary work. The illustrations are designed to place you into the mood and spirit of the work's settings.

The **MAXnotes** also include summaries, character lists, explanations of plot, and section-by-section analyses. A biography of the author and discussion of the work's historical context will help you put this literary piece into the proper perspective of what is taking place.

The use of this study guide will save you the hours of preparation time that would ordinarily be required to arrive at a complete grasp of this work of literature. You will be well prepared for classroom discussions, homework, and exams. The guidelines that are included for writing papers and reports on various topics will prepare you for any added work which may be assigned.

The **MAXnotes** will take your grades "to the max."

Dr. Max Fogiel
Program Director

Contents

> **Each Chapter includes List of Characters,**
> **Summary, Analysis, Study Questions and**
> **Answers, and Suggested Essay Topics.**

Introduction

The Life and Work of Thomas Hardy

Thomas Hardy was born June 2, 1840, in Higher Bockhampton, Dorset, England, not far from the principal settings of *Tess of the D'Urbervilles*. He was the eldest of four children. His father started a successful building and contracting business with an initial stake of only 14 pounds. His mother was Jemima Hand, who had worked as a maidservant and also had received pauper relief, a sort of welfare program. Thomas Hardy had a complicated attitude toward his family origins. He had a particular interest, common to many born into humble circumstances, in being accepted by upper-class society. Hardy was also convinced that his ancestors had formerly been successful and important but had recently come down in the world. This latter obsession parallels a belief of John Durbeyfield, the father of the heroine of *Tess of the D'Urbervilles*, that his now-poor family was once powerful and privileged.

The young Thomas was a delicate child who learned to read at about three years of age, "before he could walk." He played with the local peasant children as a young boy, but his parents forbade him to use the rural dialect spoken by many characters in *Tess*. His mother arranged for his education and tutoring, first at the village school and later at Dorchester Day School. As a teenager, Hardy taught himself Greek and began to write poetry. He wanted to become a member of the clergy, but his formal education was never advanced enough to qualify him for such a profession. Despite his eventual accomplishments, he felt ashamed of his relative lack of schooling his entire life.

At 16, Hardy was apprenticed to a Dorchester architect, John Hicks. In 1862, he left Dorchester for London to work as assistant to the architect Arthur Blomfield. While in London, he developed his intellectual tastes by attending the opera, theaters, and museums, and by reading progressive and skeptical authors such as Charles Darwin, John Stuart Mill, Herbert Spencer, and T. H. Huxley, among others.

In 1867, Hardy returned to Higher Bockhampton, and while working for John Hicks, wrote his first novel, *The Poor Man and the Lady*, now lost. The influential critic and author George Meredith advised Hardy not to publish the book, but encouraged him to write another. His second attempt at a novel, *Desperate Remedies*, was published in 1871, by William Tinsley, to mixed reviews.

Hardy soon decided to concentrate in his novels on what he knew and loved best, the social life of rural southern England. After two moderately successful novels, *Under the Greenwood Tree* (1872) and *A Pair of Blue Eyes* (1873), were published anonymously, Hardy scored a significant success in 1874 with *Far from the Madding Crowd*. After this triumph, he married Emma Lavinia Gifford, whom he had met several years earlier.

Hardy continued writing novels of "Wessex," the historical, Anglo-Saxon name he gave in fiction to his native Dorset, from this time until 1895. *Tess of the D'Urbervilles*, published in 1891, was immediately popular with the reading public. But it also caused controversy: Victorian moralists and ecclesiastics were scandalized by the author's contention that his heroine was, in the words of the novel's subtitle, a morally pure woman. In order to get the novel published in serial form, as was customary at the time, Hardy had to revise several passages considered too risqué for public consumption. For instance, the scene in which Angel Clare carries Tess and her fellow milkmaids across a stream was rewritten so as to have him instead push the women across in a wheelbarrow. Some readers were outraged by the book's pessimism, by the unrelieved picture of torment and misery Hardy presented. Orthodox believers in God were scandalized by his suggestions that the beneficent, warm God of Christianity seemed absent from the world Hardy depicted.

After the bitter denunciation of the sexual double standard in *Tess*, Hardy expanded his satiric attack in his next novel, *Jude the Obscure* (1895), which criticized the institutions of marriage and the Church and England's class system. Again, Hardy was savaged by critics who could not countenance his subversiveness. He was attacked in the press as decadent, indecent, and degenerate. (Among those offended was his wife, who took the novel as anti-religious, and thus was a blow to the devoutness she believed she shared with her husband.) Distressed by such small-mindedness, Hardy, now financially secure, vowed to give up novel-writing and return to the composition of poetry, his first literary love, which he felt would afford him greater artistic and intellectual freedom. From 1898 on, Hardy published mainly poetry. He became one of the few English authors to produce a significant body of poetry as well as novels.

After the turn of the century, he worked on *The Dynasts*, an epic-drama in verse of the Napoleonic wars, published in three volumes from 1903 to 1908. In 1910, he was awarded the Order of Merit. In 1912, he finished revising all his novels, rendering them exactly as he wanted them. In November of 1912, Emma Hardy died after a long illness, through which her husband did not give her very much aid. In 1914, Hardy married Florence Dugdale, who had been his secretary and literary aide for several years.

Hardy continued to receive honors and degrees in the first decades of the 1900s, including honorary degrees in literature from Cambridge University, in 1913, and from Oxford University, in 1920. On January 11, 1928, Thomas Hardy died. His ashes were placed in Poets' Corner of Westminster Abbey. His heart was buried in his first wife's grave, at Stinsford, next to the grave of his parents.

Historical Background

Thomas Hardy lived at a time of intense and rapid social change in England, and his novels reflect many of these changes, especially those affecting his native Wessex.

Hardy's career as a novelist roughly paralleled the late Victorian era, named after Britain's Queen Victoria, who reigned from 1837 to 1901. The Victorian period was an era of change and paradox which cannot be easily summarized. Several Victorian issues, such as economic growth and dislocation, religious and moral controversy, and the question of women's liberation, remind us of contemporary social problems.

In the first six decades of the nineteenth century, England's gross national product grew by more than 400 percent. Industrialization, which allowed for increased trade both in England and abroad, was the cause of this vast upsurge in national and, in some cases, personal wealth. Innovations in communication and travel, particularly railways, facilitated the operations of industry and the flow of money. By the end of the nineteenth century, England had become a country whose economy was based on urban industry rather than on feudal land-owning.

It is frequently said in economics that a rising tide lifts all boats—that progress and growth benefit every member of society. From personal and historical knowledge, Hardy knew this statement to contain substantial untruth. Victorian society hotly debated the ultimate value of its unprecedented economic expansion. Workers were paid more, many businessmen became rich, and England became the dominant economic power of the world, but some groups of society felt they had no place at all. Agricultural and unskilled rural workers were particularly subject to dislocation and upheaval as farmwork became less profitable than factory work. In the cities, most factory work was degrading and dangerous, and entailed living in crowded and unhealthy slums.

The demographic or population statistics tell a staggering story. The 1851 census showed that for the first time more people lived in towns and cities than the countryside, a finding that fascinated the Victorians. Over the 1800s, England's population grew from 8.9 to 32.5 million. The population of London rose sixfold over the same period, while the number of towns with a population over 50,000 went from 7 to 57. A move from the country to a city frequently meant the loss of a home and the loss of generations' worth of social traditions. One commentator, indicating the dangers of such population shifts, wrote "that the towns are gaining at the expense of the country, whose surplus population they absorb and destroy."

Another prominent feature of life in Hardy's England was a widespread loss of religious faith. In large part, this was sparked by the writings of Charles Darwin, the naturalist whose discovery of evolution put much of the Bible into serious doubt for many people. Many intellectuals abandoned their religious beliefs, including Hardy, to an extent. Denied the emotional consolation of religion, many Victorians felt that ultimate questions of human existence (Who are we? Where are we going?) were unanswerable, leaving them in confusion, feeling what Hardy calls the "ache of modernism."

Darwin's theory of the extinction of species which could not adapt to change was especially important to Hardy. Influenced by Darwin, he saw Nature and the world in unsentimental fashion, as sites of cruelty, struggle, and death. Hardy felt that classes and groups of people could become extinct if the historical conditions which supported their existence were taken away. He feared that the class his family came from, the rural laborers, might be completely destroyed if its existence was no longer useful to society. Their customs, their way of life, their style of thinking, could be lost forever—shoved aside by a new, urban bourgeois class which made a feudal-based labor system irrelevant. Hardy perceived contemporary events as part of the flow of history, driven by forces beyond individual human control.

Meanwhile, the loss of religious faith sparked general fears about a breakdown in morality. Without a foundation in religion, and without the reference point of a common religious practice, how could morality be enforced or even expected? The redistribution of wealth, power, and population effected by the Industrial Revolution combined with the atmosphere of religious doubt to lead many to conclude that England's moral fabric was being torn asunder. In *Tess of the D'Urbervilles*, Hardy uses the central characters to set up debates on the issues of religion and morality.

Another Victorian controversy of importance to *Tess* is "the Woman Question," as it was called—the issue of how women should be viewed and what roles they should play in society. Many felt that women should only work in the home, and were not capable of education or professional achievement. Some writers described the world as being made up of two spheres, the home and the public world, and tried to prove that women should be restricted to the home. Victorian women were supposed to be "an angel in the house" and nothing more. Although this was primarily a middle-class ideal, it shows the intense Victorian concern with the idea of female purity. Many Victorians felt that if a woman lost her honor, or virginity, before marriage, she was irreparably harmed, and must bear the shame the rest of her life. The plight of the so-called fallen woman was central to Victorian morality. No such prohibition was attached to male sexual behavior, and brothels thrived in the cities. The tragic effects of this double standard can be seen vividly in the life story of Tess Durbeyfield.

Master List of Characters

Tess Durbeyfield—*The heroine of the novel, a peasant girl about 16 years old at the start of the story. She is hard-working, responsible, self-possessed, serious, and extremely beautiful.*

Alec D'Urberville—*The rakish son of a rich merchant, accustomed to a life of privilege and pleasure.*

Angel Clare—*Youngest son of the Reverend Clare of Emminster. Sensitive, intellectual, and skeptical, he rejects his family's plans for him and is attempting a career as a gentleman farmer.*

John Durbeyfield—*Tess's father. Shiftless and lazy, he makes absurd plans to capitalize on his now-faded aristocratic heritage.*

Joan Durbeyfield—*Tess's mother. Superstitious, uneducated, and fatalistic, her life is guided by folk wisdom and native cunning.*

Abraham Durbeyfield—*Tess's younger brother, a boy about nine years old.*

Mrs. D'Urberville—*The blind mother of Alec, and mistress of "The Slopes," a country mansion.*

Infant Sorrow—*Tess's child by Alec D'Urberville, whom she is forced to baptize and bury without benefit of clergy.*

Izz Huett—*A milkmaid at Talbothays dairy farm, in love with Angel, and briefly the object of his attentions.*

Marian—*A milkmaid at Talbothays, in love with Angel, and later a co-worker of Tess's again.*

Car Darch—*Nicknamed Queen of Spades, coarse, aggressive, jealous woman, once linked romantically to Alec.*

Jonathan Kail—*A simple minded farmworker.*

Car Darch's Mother—*A laconic peasant with a moustache.*

Nancy Darch—*Nicknamed Queen of Diamonds, Car's sister.*

Retty Priddle—*A milkmaid at Talbothays, in love with Angel, and, like Tess, the descendant of a ruined noble family.*

Dairyman Crick—*The goodhearted owner of Talbothays dairy.*

Reverend Clare—*Angel's father, a minister, righteous, traditional, and severe, but also charitable to the unfortunate.*

Mrs. Clare—*Angel's mother, kindhearted but snobbish.*

Cuthbert and Felix Clare—*Angel's older brothers, Cuthbert a scholar and Felix a curate, who follow their father's expectations and distrust Angel because of his unorthodox lifestyle.*

Mercy Chant—*A devout and well-brought-up young girl whom Angel's parents have selected as his future wife.*

Farmer Groby—*A sullen farm manager who cruelly overworks Tess and her fellow laborers at his desolate, mechanized farm in Flintcomb-Ash.*

Liza-Lu—*A younger sister who comes to bear a striking resemblance to Tess.*

Summary of the Novel

After John Durbeyfield, a country peasant, learns he is descended from a noble family, he gets tipsy at a local alehouse. Early the next morning, Tess, his dutiful daughter, sets out to market, but she falls asleep and the family's horse dies in an accident. Tess is sent to seek work from Mrs. D'Urberville, a rich lady whom the Durbeyfields believe to be of a junior branch of the ancient family from whom they are descended. The Durbeyfields do not know that the D'Urberville name has been adopted for status purposes by a newly rich family, originally the Stokes, from the north of England. Tess's looks impress Alec Stoke-D'Urberville, who offers her a job. For several months, Alec romantically pursues Tess, finally taking her against her will in a darkened forest. She stays with him a few weeks before returning home.

Tess gives birth, but the infant soon dies, and Tess is forced to bury it herself. After a year at home, Tess becomes a milkmaid at the hospitable Talbothays Dairy, where she meets a young man who had briefly impressed her in her youth. This cultured and intellectual young man, Angel Clare, studying to be a farmer, falls in love with Tess because of her beauty and purity. Tess is reluctant, but eventually accepts the marriage and tries unsuccessfully to reveal her past before the ceremony.

The night after their wedding, Angel confesses to Tess a past liaison. Tess forgives him, but when Tess details her past, Angel is too shocked to forgive. He deserts Tess, but allows her to appeal to his parents if she has any financial troubles.

Angel sets off for Brazil to buy a farm. Tess must accept a winter job at a farm where she and her co-workers are treated brutally. Tess decides to visit Angel's parents. Before seeing them, she overhears Angel's brothers scorning his unwise marriage. On her way back, Tess hears an itinerant preacher who turns out to be Alec D'Urberville.

When he sees Tess, Alec's lust is reawakened and his religious conversion is undone. Alec again pursues Tess, offering her and her family much-needed financial help and reminding her that her husband is not acting as her protector. After her father dies and her family is rendered homeless, Tess succumbs to Alec.

Angel has been recovering from fever in Brazil, and he decides to return to England to reclaim his bride. However, when he meets her at Sandbourne, it is obvious Tess has bartered herself to D'Urberville and that Angel has arrived too late. Angel walks the streets in despair, at the same time Tess's landlord notices an ominous bloodstain, revealing that Tess has murdered Alec. Within moments the word is out and Tess is being pursued again, this time by the law. Tess and Angel spend an idyllic few days in an abandoned mansion. Trying to evade capture, they stop for the night at Stonehenge, but in the morning police surround the ancient monument and take Tess away. Her execution is witnessed only by Angel and Tess's younger sister.

Structure of the Novel

The novel is unified by the simple aim of telling every important event in Tess's life from the age of 16 to her death when she is about 23 years old. It is Tess's book—virtually every scene features her, or includes her as the object of discussion. The book has aspects of a *Bildungsroman*, or novel of individual development, and also has the design of a tragedy.

Hardy uses no experimental or confusing narrative devices. There is a pleasure in being able to identify and respond to all the elements of a story, and Hardy fully allows this pleasure in *Tess of the D'Urbervilles*. We immediately recognize the role the main characters play in the story: Tess is an exemplary heroine, with whom we empathize and suffer; Alec is introduced as a villain; and Angel is a lover and, as his name indicates, a possible savior for Tess. Except for one or two moments, the characters always act consistently with what we know about them. When we understand the story so clearly, our sentiments and emotions are readily engaged. The emotional power of the novel is reflected by our pity at Tess's suffering, our anger at those who let her down, and our awe at her almost superhuman endurance.

What primarily interests Hardy in *Tess* is the juxtaposition of a remarkable series of events. He creates an elaborate web of coincidence, accident, fate, history, and just plain bad luck that seems to doom Tess no matter how she acts or what she does. As in classical tragedy, the universe itself conspires against human effort, no matter how noble, and against human happiness, no matter how greatly sought after. In his later poetry, Hardy defined the universe as being guided not by God or human design but instead by an indifferent or evil force he called the Immanent Will. This Will works silently and relentlessly against the efforts of humans and the human race.

Thomas Hardy unifies and amplifies his novel with detailed descriptions of landscapes and incidents from Nature. He describes Tess's psychological states by writing about the physical places she inhabits. Thus her tortured mind and feelings that she is being pursued are presented to us in visual form, as in the elaborate description, painted through words, of a night she must sleep amidst a group of injured pheasants. Similarly, the two farms where she works can be compared and contrasted. While describing Talbothays Dairy, Hardy emphasizes color, growth, and fertility; while showing us Flintcomb-Ash, he communicates the bleakness and danger of Tess's situation in terms of a desolate, barren, cold environment.

Hardy also threads a series of color references throughout the novel. The careful reader will note repeated references to the colors of red and white. White symbolizes innocence and purity; red indicates experience, violation, danger, and death.

It is important to note that *Tess of the D'Urbervilles* is the story, not just of an individual, but of her class. Just as Tess's personal fortunes decline, so does the economic and social position of her family, and the class to which it belongs. Hardy charts and explains a number of steps in a steady downward progression of the rural class into which Tess is born.

Estimated Reading Time

To Hardy's original Victorian audience, reading long novels either to oneself or aloud to family and friends was a customary form of entertainment. The novel was first presented serially and was published weekly from July to December, 1891, in a popular magazine, the *Graphic*. Hardy's final version of the novel is divided into seven Phases. Each Phase builds to an exceptional high or low point in Tess's life. You can carefully read each Phase in a sitting of two or three hours, noting the actions and personalities of important characters, and the shifts in Tess's fortunes and happiness. The entire novel can be read in about 20 hours.

For the analytical purposes of this study guide and to aid your comprehension of all the novel's important details, several Phases have been divided into two parts.

Tess of the D'Urbervilles

Phase the First: The Maiden
Chapters 1–4

New Characters:

Parson Tringham: *a parson who studies ancient English history*

John Durbeyfield: *a country peddler, inclined neither to serious-ness nor hard work*

Tess Durbeyfield: *a beautiful country girl, "a mere vessel of emo-tion untinctured by experience"*

The club-women of Marlott: *a group of local women enjoying a ritual May-Day dance*

Joan Durbeyfield: *Tess's mother, superstitious and eager for escape from her daily grind*

Abraham Durbeyfield: *Tess's younger brother*

Eliza-Louisa Durbeyfield: *Tess's younger sister, nicknamed Liza–Lu*

Mrs. Rolliver: *the proprietor of a local alehouse*

Angel, Cuthbert, and Felix: *three brothers, upper-class young gentle-men on a walking tour*

The mail-cart man: *the unwitting perpetrator of a fatal accident*

Summary

John Durbeyfield, a poor country haggler, is met on the road to his Marlott home by Parson Tringham. The Parson, against his better judgment, lets slip that John is actually descended from a noble family, the D'Urbervilles, which first came to England with William the Conqueror and which controlled much land and power in the area. On the strength of this news, Durbeyfield's self-esteem is greatly elevated, and he decides to stop off at Rolliver's Inn for some drinks.

In Chapter Two, Hardy shifts the scene to the town of Marlott, in the vale of Blackmoor—a fertile place unvisited by many from the outside world. John's daughter Tess, a beautiful girl about 16 years old, is participating in the Marlott custom of a May-Day dance. She sees her father drunkenly boasting about his ancestry, and speaks curtly to her friends who tease her about him. While at the dance, an interesting-looking young gentleman, not from the area, is seen by Tess. Before he has a chance to dance with her, he must leave to rejoin his brothers.

After his drinking, and because of his poor health, Tess's father is unable to drive the family cart with its load of beehives to Casterbridge market, and Tess volunteers for the duty, bringing along her younger brother Abraham so she can stay awake. Abraham asks about the stars, and Tess explains their family's poverty by saying they live on a "blighted" or decaying planet. Soon, both doze off and their horse, Prince, is rammed by the mail cart and dies, splattering Tess with his blood. Tess feels responsible for Prince's death, which imperils the family's livelihood.

Joan Durbeyfield, Tess's mother, has heard that there is a rich woman by the name of D'Urberville living not far off in the town of Trantridge. Joan reasons that Tess can, on the basis of their supposed family connection, get a job there, as a way of helping the family finances.

Analysis

The chain of coincidences and disastrous accidents which entraps Tess begins with the very first scene of the novel. The episodes of the novel are set in a straight, forward line, with minimal digressions or flashbacks. The story of Tess's sufferings originates

from the chance meeting of Parson Tringham and John Durbey-field, the first scene of the novel. Hardy reminds us later several times that if this meeting had not occurred, everything which fol-lowed (Durbeyfield getting drunk, the horse dying, Tess having to appeal to the fake D'Urbervilles) might not have happened the fate-ful, disastrous way it did. The novel takes the shape of an unbreak-able set of causes and effects, each event leading irrevocably onto the next, as if things were fated to be thus and no other way for Tess. Noting this structure, an early critic wrote, in an appropriate natural metaphor, "The sequence of lightning and thunder is not more prompt than that of cause and effect in Mr. Hardy's story."

The pattern of suffering is laid out for Tess by the operations of the world, but is made inevitable by the core elements of Tess's personality, especially the admirable ones. Her tragedy is one of individual conscience. Tess is a rarity in literature—a good charac-ter, protective, loyal, hardworking, moral, and innocent. Her re-sponsibility and diligence are continually compared to the shiftlessness of her parents in these early chapters. Tess is extremely protective of her parents, her siblings, and the reputation of her family. When her friends mock her father, Tess curtly stops them; when he later is too tipsy to drive, she does so in order to hide her father's state from the rest of the town. Tess's behavior and thoughts are always concerned with others: she bemoans the sorry plight of her family, and she feels she must do something about it. Within the space of a few pages, we read several references to the strength of her conscience. She feels self-reproach when thinking about not helping her mother with the chores; she has a sting of remorse that she has dirtied her white dress; and she feels shame at the rather childlike, indulgent behavior of her parents. The rest of the novel gives Tess many more occasions to experience such feelings.

It is important to note that Hardy introduces his heroine as a product of her native village, Marlott, and its natural setting, the Vale of Blackmoor. The Vale is elaborately described as a fertile and sheltered tract of country, in which the fields are never brown and the springs never dry. There, the world seems to be constructed upon a smaller and more delicate scale.

Hardy describes Tess's home environment as a protected place, fertile, connected to nature, and almost a world of its own.

Its beauty, vulnerability, and fragility implicitly become characteristics of Tess, who becomes nearly a personification of her native Wessex. Tess herself is first described as one of a group of similar-looking country women, dressed in white and adorned with flowers; all of these women seem shy and self-conscious. What distinguishes Tess physically is her beauty, her youth, her adolescent face, and the red ribbon in her hair. This last detail is the first instance of the red-and-white motif that is woven into the novel.

We are not given a head-to-toe physical description of Tess. Hardy relies on a description of her lips and mouth, using the literary device of metonymy, the substitution of the part for the whole, to communicate Tess's superlative beauty. By not supplying a complete description, Hardy invites his readers to form their own mental images of Tess.

The second most important character in the book, Angel, whose last name is not revealed until later, is briefly glimpsed by both Tess and the reader in the club-walking scene. Angel's looks and manner and his failure to notice Tess until just before he has to leave the dance sets the tone for their entire relationship. Angel's class superiority to the Marlott villagers is underlined by Hardy— it is as if he is a tourist from another country.

Hardy takes care to define the historical backgrounds as well as the geographical and social positions of his characters. He wishes us to know it is the Victorian era, and he wants us to see the impact this era will make on the lives of his characters. The walking-tour brothers mention a prominent religious conflict of the day. The Vale of Blackmoor is geographically close to but culturally distant from the great urban center of London. Joan's use of the *Compleat Fortune-Teller* tells us something of her social background.

The most explicit reference to the cultural atmosphere of the Victorian age is contained in this comparison of Tess and Joan: "Between the mother, with her fast-perishing lumber of superstition, folk-lore, dialect, and orally transmitted ballads, and the daughter, with her trained National teachings and Standard knowledge under an infinitely Revised code, there was a gap of two hundred years as ordinarily understood." When they were together, the Jacobean and the Victorian ages were juxtaposed.

It is easy to condemn and make fun of Joan and John, who are mentally limited and often foolish, but an unreserved condemnation of them is not quite fair, and not exactly what Hardy wanted. Joan always acts within the context of the traditional beliefs and customs with which she was raised. Her daughter, growing up when public education is becoming more widespread, has been exposed to new and contemporary ways of thinking, and has a greater fund of rational knowledge available to her. Both Joan and Tess are shaped by what they were taught during the historical eras in which they were raised.

The trip to Casterbridge that Tess makes with Abraham provides Hardy an opportunity to introduce the theme of random fate running a cruel world. When young Abraham begins to tire, "He leant back against the hives, and with upturned face made observations on the stars, whose cold pulses were beating amid the black hollows above in serene dissociation from these two wisps of human life. He asked how far away those twinklers were, and whether God was on the other side of them." Abraham asks an innocent, childlike question about the sky. Hardy portrays a universe that does not care about human doings. Hardy implies that God, if He exists, also seems remote or indifferent. The theme of the world as inhospitable recurs constantly in the novel.

The accident with Prince follows this conversation, and Tess shows her sense of responsibility and self-reproach again. She has a far greater understanding of what the death of Prince means than do any others in her family, and she feels that she is fully and totally at fault. Nobody blamed Tess as she blamed herself. She looks at herself as if she was a murderess. Her sense of obligation makes her feel she must obey her parents' plans to repair the damage done to the family business.

Hardy shows several representative facets of his prose style in these first chapters. Three important techniques used here are his concern with capturing the rural dialect in writing; his allusive and complex sentences and vocabulary; and his communication of the mood or atmosphere of a scene through a description of its setting.

The first technique, Hardy's goal of replicating peasant speech, was of great interest to his contemporary readers, many of whom

were urban and intrigued by experiencing an unfamiliar style of English. To modern readers, this goal may not seem as compelling.

Hardy's complicated vocabulary and allusive references were sometimes criticized by Victorian reviewers. Their plaint, shared by many modern readers, is that Hardy chooses unfamiliar and complex words that can become distracting and hard to under-stand, and that his sentences can be too ornately designed for easy comprehension. Hardy's vocabulary can be overly difficult; at other times he is committed to using the full reach of the En-glish language to illustrate fine distinctions and subtle points. An example of Hardy's high-blown diction is this sentence concern-ing Joan Durbeyfield's mental capacities: "Troubles and other re-alities took on themselves a metaphysical impalpability, sinking to mere mental phenomena for serene contemplation, and no longer stood as pressing concretions which chafed body and soul." The sentence aims for a precise description of the way Joan's mind makes real-life problems less difficult. The thought may be hard to perceive because of its philosophical generality and its complex diction.

Hardy's allusions to history and to literature also deepen and complicate his prose. Thomas Hardy was always fond of referring to classical literature, and he does so repeatedly in Tess. A small example in Chapter Two is his portrait of Angel: "there was an uncribbed, uncabined aspect in his eyes and attire." The two ad-jectives, "uncribbed, uncabined," refer to a description of Macbeth in Shakespeare's play of that name as cribbed and cabined, that is, bound in by fears and restrictions—Angel is apparently just the opposite. The allusion, while subtle, shows Hardy assuming his readers will be able to pick up on the reference to England's most famous writer.

Another significant mode of allusion in Hardy is to history, especially classical and ancient history. "The club of Marlott alone lived to uphold the local Cerealia," Hardy writes of the club-walk-ing. He means that in this local May-Day dance we are seeing a continuation of an ancient celebration of earthly fertility that goes back to the holidays of classical Greece. Hardy makes us reflect on the historical distance and the historical continuity between the modern and the ancient eras.

Throughout the novel, Hardy depicts mood (emotional or mental conditions) through setting (physical descriptions). This correlation is a hallmark of Hardy's style. When Tess scolds her mother for letting John go out drinking, "Her [Tess's] rebuke and her mood seemed to fill the whole room, and to impart a cowed look to the furniture, and candle, and children playing about, and to her mother's face."

Hardy chooses not to analyze or describe Tess's mood, but to show it visually in terms of her environment. The scene at Rolliver's Inn also uses imagery and description. "The stage of mental comfort to which they had arrived at this hour was one wherein their souls expanded beyond their skins, and spread their personalities warmly through the room. In this process the chamber and its furniture grew more and more dignified and luxurious; the shawl hanging at the window took upon itself the richness of tapestry; the brass handles of the chest of drawers were as golden knockers; and the carved bed-posts seemed to have some kinship with the magnificent pillars of Solomon's temple." The matching of personality to environment can be noted time and again by attentive readers of Hardy.

Study Questions

1. How does John Durbeyfield learn about his true family heritage?

2. What is the name of the valley where Tess and her family live?

3. What distinguishes Tess from her fellow country maidens?

4. What happens at the first meeting between Tess and Angel?

5. What do the two older brothers on a walking tour wish to do, instead of dancing with local girls?

6. Who takes care of the children in the Durbeyfield family?

7. What happens on the road to Casterbridge market?

8. What is the subject of Tess's and Abraham's conversation as they ride to market?

9. What does Joan Durbeyfield rely on when deciding Tess's future plans?

10. Why does Tess consent to her mother's plan that she ask Mrs. D'Urberville for a job?

Answers

1. On impulse, a local man gives this information to John Durbeyfield as they meet by chance on a country road.

2. The Durbeyfield's home village is in the vale (or valley) of Blakemore or Blackmoor.

3. Tess's beauty sets her apart from her friends. She is the only girl in the procession adorned with a red ribbon.

4. Angel, drawn by curiosity, dances with a local woman at Marlott's May-Day procession. Tess sees Angel and is impressed by his distinguished manner and looks. Angel sees Tess and is momentarily regretful he did not dance with her.

5. The two older brothers wish to have time later on to discuss a book dealing with a contemporary religious controversy, the rise of atheism.

6. Tess is the oldest child by more than four years, and the hardest-working member of the family. Much of the child-care responsibility goes to her.

7. Abraham and Tess fall asleep early in the morning as their horse, Prince, drags a cart loaded up with beehives to market in Casterbridge. Walking on the wrong side of the road, Prince is gored by the mail cart, and dies.

8. Tess describes how humans live on a "blighted star," thus accounting for the miserable position of the Durbeyfield family.

9. Joan relies on a book, the *Compleat Fortune-Teller*, to predict Tess's future.

10. "Nobody blamed Tess as she blamed herself" for the death of Prince. Her guilt over this accident and her sense of responsibility for her family override her intuition that the project of "claiming kin" with the D'Urbervilles is unwise.

Suggested Essay Topics

1. One of Hardy's concerns in the novel is to describe the customs and manners of England's rural life, which he felt were being lost to industrialization and modernization. What descriptions and incidents in the first four chapters build a picture of rural life in the late nineteenth century?

2. What parts do Fate, Chance, and sheer accident play in the beginning of Tess's life story?

3. How is Tess contrasted to her parents?

4. How does Hardy make Tess appear as a representative example of her native environment and her gender?

Phase the First: The Maiden
Chapters 5–11

New Characters:

Alec Stoke-D'Urberville: *the young son of a wealthy merchant, a dashing, gallant, forceful ladies' man*

Mrs. D'Urberville: *an eccentric blind widow and the reluctantly loving mother of Alec*

Car Darch: *nicknamed Queen of Spades, coarse, aggressive, jealous woman, once linked romantically to Alec.*

Nancy Darch: *nicknamed the Queen of Diamonds, Car's sister, also a former favorite of D'Urberville*

Car Darch's mother: *a laconic peasant woman with a moustache*

Summary

Tess is pressured by her mother to approach Mrs. D'Urberville, a rich lady living not far from Marlott. The Durbeyfields believe she is of a junior branch of the D'Urberville family and thus will render the Durbeyfields some material assistance in their time of need. Tess undertakes an initial visit to see Mrs. D'Urberville.

Tess is unsettled by what she sees at the D'Urberville manor, an estate called The Slopes. The house does not fit into its environment; it has been built solely for pleasure and not at all for agricultural functionality. "Everything looked like money—like the last coin issued from the Mint." The manor exists primarily to show off the wealth of its nouveau riche owners. Tess is disappointed that when she sees the son of the family, Alec D'Urberville, he compares unfavorably to the mental picture she had of her "D'Urberville" relatives as dignified, ancient, and bearing traces of their illustrious past.

Alec announces that his invalid mother cannot see Tess, but that he might be able to help her. Tess feels that her appeal for aid must sound foolish but manages to explain her family's financial need, occasioned, she admits, by her killing the family's horse. Alec's roving eye lights upon Tess's beauty, her "luxuriance of aspect," and he keeps her on the estate for a few hours, feeding her freshly-picked strawberries and adorning her with roses.

Tess travels home to report on the visit but finds a letter offering her a job tending the estate's fowls has preceded her arrival. The letter appears to be in a masculine handwriting. Tess has misgivings, but for the sake of the family, she decides to take the job.

Two days later, Alec D'Urberville arrives for Tess and her belongings. Joan and her children follow along to the edge of town, where Joan has a fleeting moment of doubt about the path on which she has set her daughter.

Alec angers Tess by driving too fast down an incline, which forces Tess to put her arms around Alec so as not to fall out of the carriage. When Tess criticizes Alec, he shows a flash of anger. Alec asks to place just "one little kiss on those holmberry lips." Tess capitulates icily, offering her cheek to Alec, and he gives her "the kiss of mastery." To avoid further close contact, Tess lets her hat blow off and will not remount the carriage after picking it up. She angrily walks the rest of the way to The Slopes as Alec drives the carriage alongside her.

Once working at The Slopes, Tess is surprised to learn that Mrs. D'Urberville is blind. She never learns that Mrs. D'Urberville has not heard of their supposed family relation. Tess does her best to fit in and do a good job tending the fowl. Mrs. D'Urberville assigns

Tess the odd job of whistling to her pet bullfinches to keep them entertained. Alec, attracted to Tess but biding his time, teaches Tess to whistle.

After several weeks of working, Tess is persuaded to go to a dance one Saturday night in the nearby town of Trantridge. She has been up working since early in the morning and is physically exhausted. When her friends consent to leave the dance, an unfortunate accident results in everyone laughing at Car Darch, a woman who was once favored with D'Urberville's affections. Car and her sister, Nancy, start a fight with Tess. Along rides Alec D'Urberville, who offers Tess an escape via his carriage. Feeling pleased to remove herself from danger, Tess climbs in.

Alec rides in circles through the dark night, tracing an aimless path through the Chase, in order to spend more time with Tess. He asks to be treated as a lover (suitor) by Tess, but she evades this demand. Alec informs her that her brothers and sisters have new toys and her father a new cob. Tess is embarrassed by having to be grateful to D'Urberville. Eventually, he admits he is lost and stops his horse. He gives his overcoat to Tess as he goes off to find his bearings. When he returns, Tess is asleep. When Alec discovers this fact, he takes her bodily. Tess is without any protector. Her suffering has started, and a "chasm" separates her past from her future life.

Analysis

Throughout these chapters, Hardy continues to emphasize Tess's highly developed senses of diligence and responsibility towards her family. Tess is both the oldest daughter and the only functioning parent in the Durbeyfield clan. Everyone else in the family is a "waiter upon Providence"; that is, they prefer to hope that God or fate will provide them some help, instead of having the initiative to better their situation through their own efforts. In contrast to such shiftlessness, Tess's principal, and frequently mentioned, motivation in this early part of the novel is to make enough money so that the family can buy a new horse and re-establish their business.

Each time she questions the idea of appealing to the D'Urbervilles for help, she remembers that, because she was responsible for the death of Prince, she must make amends and has no right to

dispute her parents' plans. Such renunciation of her own misgivings culminates in a famous moment of passivity, in which Tess consents to be dressed up by her mother for the journey to Trantridge, saying "Do what you will with me, mother." All too eagerly, Joan cleans Tess up and adorns her with a large ribbon. It is as if Tess is made pretty prior to being offered up as a sort of sacrifice. Joan views her daughter's beautiful face as an asset in securing a marriage with these rich relatives. Though Joan vulgarly exploits her daughter for her own financial benefit, she has, of course, no idea of the villainous behavior Alec will deal to Tess.

Lionel Johnson, a nineteenth-century scholar on Hardy's writing, defined his principal theme as one of "urban invasion": the destruction of rural Southern England and its way of life by the economic power of industrial, urbanized North England. *Tess* fits this theme. Simon Stoke, Alec Stoke-D'Urberville's recently deceased father, made a fortune in the North of England, either as a merchant or as a money-lender—the narrator professes indecision on this point. Whatever his means of becoming rich, Stoke feels that his newly acquired money allows him to set himself up as a country man of leisure and to be addressed not by the common name of his birth but by a more exalted one. Stoke comes upon an ancient, historical name once common in Wessex, and simply appropriates it for his own use as if having money means he can lay claim to a more distinguished, socially esteemed past.

The scene of Tess's first encounter with Alec presents us with several striking and memorable visual images. In addition to providing interesting plot and characters, Hardy frequently concentrates on describing visual moments. Two such images are Alec feeding Tess strawberries, and Tess, bedecked with roses, being pricked by their thorns. While such events are important as plot, they are also meant to present images that can be fixed in our minds.

Although Tess's behavior in the strawberry scene may seem oddly unquestioning, we should remember that a certain dreamy disconnection from reality has already marked the behavior of Joan (with her eagerness for drunken relief from degrading actuality) and John (with his wild schemes for re-asserting his aristocratic heritage). Hardy draws our attention several times to his belief in heredity as a force in human character. To Hardy, traits, behaviors, and personality features can be passed down from parent to child. Thus, when she eats the strawberries "as one in a dream," in a "half-pleased, half-reluctant" condition, Tess is exhibiting behavior consistent with her Durbeyfield lineage. She herself has also been described as "lost in a vague interspace between a dream" and the real world, and it is her "reverie" which leads to her falling asleep prior to the accident with Prince.

Chapter Five closes with a famous passage in which the narrator adopts an Olympian distance from current events and speculates on the tragedy and mischance that will characterize Tess's life from the point of her meeting with D'Urberville. Hardy tells us that Fate is conspiring against Tess and her chances for happiness. From the standpoint of infinite knowledge of the future, he lets us know that things will get far worse for Tess; what looks like just another day is truly a portent of disaster: "Thus the thing began. Had she perceived this meeting's import she might have asked why she was doomed to be seen and coveted that day by the wrong man, and not by some other man, the right and desired one in all respects— as nearly as humanity can supply the right and desired...In the ill-judged execution of the well-judged plan of things the call seldom produces the comer, the man to love rarely coincides with the hour for loving. Nature does not often say 'See!' to her poor creature at a time when seeing can lead to happy doing...in the present case, as in millions, it was not the two halves of a perfect whole that confronted each other at the perfect moment; a missing counterpart wandered independently about the earth waiting in crass obtuseness till the late time came." Tess Durbeyfield is the doomed plaything of a cosmic irony, a tragic victim of pre-ordained mistiming.

Hardy's language reveals that Tess's tragedy lies beyond social causality: "We may wonder whether at the acme and summit of human progress these anachronisms will be corrected by a finer intuition, a closer interaction of the social machinery than that which now jolts us around and along; but such completeness is not to be prophesied, or even conceived as possible." Tragedy, mischance, and unhappiness cannot be corrected by tinkering with the standards, morality, or procedures of society. The probability of misery inheres in life itself.

Yet throughout the novel, Hardy makes clear also that the social and historical environment—the particular conditions of late nineteenth-century, rural England—aid Tess's downfall. The lack of need for Durbeyfield's occupation in a changing economic order puts his family at the financial mercy of the Stoke-D'Urberville family, which is representative of the new, sometimes unscrupulous business classes then rising in Victorian England. Tess is a poor, relatively uneducated woman, who is limited in her options for making money, and is placed at the mercy of the men with whom she must deal.

Tragedy usually requires an inevitable cause, some force which unalterably opposes human possibility. A problem for the reader of *Tess* is to determine the one inevitable cause of Tess's tragedy. Hardy is not always clear about which factors are the most influential in Tess's life-story, and which are most responsible for her apparently foreordained and unalterable misery. Is it her struggle against a cruel social and economic system in which, as a young, poor, innocent woman, she cannot find a position guaranteeing her safety from a powerful rich man like D'Urberville? Or is this historical, social reading a sort of red herring or false clue, and her struggle is simply one against a cruel world, actively set against the possibilities of human happiness? Hardy suggests one perspective and then others.

Hardy does not take us very far into Alec's past or psychology. How Alec got to be Alec, in short, is left unexplained: he simply is what he is. Readers are not left in suspense over his villainous role in Tess's story. The innocent Tess cannot guess what Hardy tells us, that Alec was "potentially the 'tragic mischief' of her drama—one who stood fair to be the blood-red ray in the spectrum of her life." That he is a gallant or a lover is apparent from his first words: "Well, my Beauty, what can I do for you?" His reputation as a "gallant," or a lady-killer who pursues his desires in a self-centered fashion, is already well-established in the Trantridge area. He exhibits a casual air of command, an ease with the power, particularly that over women, that his social and economic position gives him.

Chapter 11 provides a famous example of the Hardy narrative style and language at its best. The steady accumulation of physical detail about Tess's fatigue, early in the chapter, leads into the poetic evocation of the dark, silent, isolated forest. Alec shows the full range of his behavior, moving from male self-confidence to class arrogance (calling Tess a mere chit) to a brutally timed reminder of his generosity to Tess's family. Forces of all sorts trap Tess. Poised above the pair, writes Hardy, are "gentle roosting birds in their last nap." Like these birds, Tess is sleeping and vulnerable.

"Where was Tess's guardian angel?" Hardy goes on to ask. Of course she has none and will never have one. God, or some other force which should protect the innocent, seems to be absent from at least this part of the world. Or perhaps the God above Tess simply has better things to do: He might be talking, or taking a trip, or sleeping. Alec's appropriation (a word with legal connotations of theft) of Tess's innocence is inexplicable by any morality. In the face of such unaccountable divergence of the ideal from the actual, the only appropriate comment might be the fatalistic folk wisdom Hardy quotes: "It was to be." The disasters of life cannot be explained, only endured.

Study Questions

1. What tips the balance of Tess's decision as to whether to approach Mrs. D'Urberville?

2. What is the name of the home of Mrs. D'Urberville?

3. Why has Simon Stoke decided to rename himself D'Urberville?

4. What job is Tess given by the D'Urbervilles?

5. How is Tess dressed when her parents send her off?

6. What is the mother-son relationship of Mrs. D'Urberville and Alec like?

7. What does Alec teach Tess how to do?

8. What defect marks the social life of the people in and around Trantridge?

9. Who picks a fight with Tess on the way home from Chaseborough, and why?

10. What happens in The Chase?

Answers

1. Her guilt over the death of Prince, combined with her feeling that she is responsible for the family, cause Tess finally to agree to the idea of applying to Mrs. D'Urberville for help.

2. The manorial home of Mrs. D'Urberville is named The Slopes.

3. Simon Stoke has earned a fortune as a merchant, or perhaps as a moneylender, in the industrialized north of England. Stoke does not want to be associated with his unprestigious (or shady) past, and he believes that an aristocratic name would be more distinguished than his original one. He found the name D'Urberville in a history book dealing with old families in the south of England.

4. Tess is assigned the job of tending to a group of fowl kept by Mrs. D'Urberville. She must feed, care for, and entertain these birds.

5. Tess is dressed in a white muslin dress and her newly washed hair is tied with a large red ribbon.

6. Mrs. D'Urberville is not ignorant of her son's faults, but nevertheless loves him. She is "bitterly fond" of Alec.

7. Alec teaches Tess how to whistle so that she can keep Mrs. D'Urberville's birds happy.

8. The villagers around Trantridge live for the moment, disdaining the idea of saving for the future. Many of them are hard drinkers.

9. The Darch sisters, jealous that Alec is now smitten with Tess instead of them, pick a fight with her.

10. Unheedful of the route home, Alec drives his carriage until his horse is exhausted. He deposits Tess in a portion of The Chase and goes to look for directions. When he comes back, he ascertains Tess is asleep, and takes her.

Suggested Essay Topics

1. Research the historical phenomenon of newly rich families buying titles or adopting aristocratic names in Victorian

England. How common were such practices? How closely in accordance with these historical facts is Hardy's fictional presentation of Simon Stoke?

2. Thomas Hardy frequently indicates which of his characters he morally approves of by describing their attitude to hard work. Pick three characters from Phase the First and analyze how Hardy judges them by portraying their differing attitudes to work and labor. Devote one paragraph to each character and include several quotes from the novel in each paragraph. Write an introductory paragraph with an appropriately worded thesis statement and end the essay with a conclusion restating your findings and assessing their importance.

3. At two important moments in Chapters Five and 11, Hardy departs from describing events and shifts into an omniscient narrative voice which makes philosophical pronouncements. How do these shifts of narrative voice add to our experience of the novel?

4. Literary critics frequently describe characters as being either round or flat. Round characters are constantly changing, evolving, maturing, presenting new, unpredictable aspects to readers. Flat characters are defined more in terms of several focused and unchanging characteristics, making them easily memorable but not, perhaps, so interesting for the reader to spend time with. (The English novelist E. M. Forster formulated this distinction in his book *Aspects of the Novel*, published in 1927, a number of years after Hardy wrote *Tess*.) Assess whether Tess, Alec D'Urberville, Angel Clare, or Joan Durbeyfield are round or flat characters. Can a flat character compel our interest?

5. How many times does the thought of Prince's death affect Tess's behavior? Describe how Tess constantly shows responsibility for the well-being and reputation of her family.

Phase the Second: Maiden No More
Chapters 12–15

New Characters:

The Sign-painter: *a man whose evangelical messages unsettle our heroine*

The Parson: *a vicar whose adherence to established rules nearly outweighs his true religious feelings*

Infant Sorrow: *Tess's child by Alec D'Urberville, whom she is forced to baptize and bury without benefit of clergy.*

Summary

Several weeks after the night in the Chase, Tess walks home to Marlott, "her views of life" having been "totally changed" by recent experiences. D'Urberville catches up to her in a carriage and offers to ride her home if she is not willing to return to him at Trantridge. Tess refuses to continue being Alec's "creature," and turns down his offers of financial help. Alec reiterates these offers, especially "if certain circumstances arise," an allusion Tess does not pick up on. Alec then bids good-bye to his "four months' cousin."

Shortly after this encounter, Tess is overtaken by a man whose avocation is to paint Bible verses on walls in the countryside. After reading his oddly punctuated message, "THY, DAMNATION, SLUMBERETH, NOT," Tess feels horror and shame that this man seems to know her sinfulness.

At home, Tess first speaks with her mother, who is surprised and upset that Tess does not intend to get Alec to marry her. Joan tells her daughter she should have been more careful if she did not want Alec's affections to lead to marriage. Tess replies that her mother had not informed her of the danger men represent to women. Despite her disappointment that Tess has ruined a good chance for the family's advancement, Joan soon is resigned to what her daughter has done, and vows to "make the best of it."

A few friends visit, and their envy of Tess's romantic conquest of D'Urberville lifts her spirits, but only temporarily. A few weeks

later she attends church, but the whispering of the congregants convinces Tess she is not welcome even there. To avoid such gossipy disapproval, Tess takes long walks at night, hiding herself from the eyes of her fellow villagers while contemplating her own guilt.

By next harvest time, Tess has ended her isolation and participates in the work of reaping wheat. One day at noon Tess nurses her baby in the fields, but later that afternoon it is apparent that the baby, never large or healthy, is now sick and dying. Tess realizes she must get the baby baptized, but her father, inflamed again by pride over his knightly roots, and not wishing anyone to meddle in his domestic affairs, refuses to let the parson in the house. Tess improvises a baptismal ceremony, enlisting the prayers of her younger siblings. Shortly after, the baby dies. When Tess sees the parson, he says Tess's baptism will save the baby's soul, but he initially balks at the idea of the baby being buried in consecrated ground. (The baby is buried in a corner of the graveyard.)

Tess remains in isolation all winter, until she realizes that she could never be comfortable in a place which knew about her recent history. Hearing of a summer job at a dairy, coincidentally located not far from her D'Urberville family seat, Tess vows to start a new life there.

Analysis

Phase the Second functions as a transition between Tess's experiences with Alec and her later life. The title of the Phase gives a sense of the changes Tess is going through physically, spiritually, and psychologically. It is important to realize that Hardy uses the idea of Tess being a "Maiden No More" in a double sense.

In one meaning, Tess is no longer a maiden in the technical, Victorian sense of the term: she is no longer a virgin, having been Alec D'Urberville's lover. By such reasoning, Tess is a completely different person who no longer can be accorded the respect given to an untouched or a married woman.

Hardy describes Tess's neighbors in Marlott as making her feel unwelcome at church, where their humanitarian feelings should be most engaged. Hardy uses the language of Victorian morality only to critique it. He wishes to transvalue or transform the idea that Tess has become a different person and to put in a different context the notion that she is guilty and to be looked down on, morally and socially.

In this more positive sense, Tess is a "Maiden No More" because her experiences have altered her sensations, her perspectives, and her knowledge of the world. She is now a woman and not a child, not merely because she is not a virgin, but because she has painfully accumulated knowledge of life's dangers and burdens.

Hardy's depiction of Tess as a seduced, abandoned maiden differs radically from the treatment of this same theme in Victorian literature. This difference resides mainly in the fact that Hardy refuses to explicitly criticize his heroine. Instead, his emotions become fully engaged in sympathizing with her. A frequent fate of fictional women engaging in illicit sex in Victorian literature was to commit suicide when they could no longer bear their shame. Hardy's emotional commitment to and respect for the spiritual purity of Tess, no matter what she does or what people may think of it, is developed in this Phase. Hardy's depiction of Tess in the baptism scene shows how much Hardy feels for and approves of his heroine. Her face, he writes, acquires a "touch of dignity which was almost regal." She pours forth thanksgiving "from the bottom of her heart...uttering it boldly and triumphantly." Hardy seems to be so enamoured of Tess's beauty and dignity that he momentarily forgets she is only a character he has created.

Hardy is careful to note that the moral disapproval which Tess feels does not solely come from society or other people. Tess's conscience functions as her most powerful critic. Her consciousness that she is guilty and sinful is great, and, in Hardy's opinion, much greater than it needs to be. When looked at within the context of natural life, which implies the necessity of growth and generation, her activities have been normal and unexceptionable, not sinful or shameful. "Walking among the sleeping birds in the hedges, watching the skipping rabbits on a moonlit warren, or standing under a pheasant-laden bough, she looked upon herself as a figure of Guilt intruding into the haunts of Innocence. But all the while she was making a distinction where there was no difference. Feeling herself in antagonism, she was quite in accord. She had been made to break an accepted social law, but no law known to the environment in which she fancied herself such an anomaly." The conventional disapproval Tess feels so keenly is nothing more than a creation of her fancy, "a cloud of moral hobgoblins" with no foundation in the realest of worlds, the natural one.

Phase the Second contains two sections with themes characteristic of Hardy's deepest aims as a novelist. The first section is an extended description of fieldwork and the relationship of farm workers to their environment. Hardy includes many details about how reaping was done at Tess's time, while his descriptions also emphasize Tess's sense of capability and satisfaction in doing such traditional work. The other notable section, dealing with the makeshift baptism and burial of infant Sorrow, critiques the practice of organized religion in England as deficient to the ideals of what true religion should be. The sneering tone in his comment about the parson is unmistakable: "Having the natural feelings of a tradesman at finding that a job he should have been called in for had been unskillfully botched by his customers...he was disposed to say no" to Tess's questions about the efficacy of Sorrow's baptism. This vicar cannot recognize authentic spirituality when it is in front of his face. He apparently believes that true religious feeling is allowed only to those whose job it is to be religious.

Hardy does not describe any of the events that occur between the night in The Chase and Tess's return to Marlott, and his presentation of the encounter in The Chase is oblique and indirect. Thus, we are left with difficulty in determining what has happened between Tess and Alec and are uncertain about how much Tess truly acceded to Alec's pursuit of her. Did she want or accept this sexual relationship at any time, or was it always something forced on her by D'Urberville? Was the incident in The Chase a seduction or a rape? Tess never speaks of it as such, though some farm workers quoted in this Phase believe or have heard that "A little more than persuading had to do wi'...it." The narrator puts it in a slightly different way: "She had...succumbed to adroit advantages he took of her helplessness; then, temporarily blinded by his ardent manners, had been stirred to confused surrender awhile: had suddenly despised and disliked him, and had run away." It is thus apparent that the liaison went on for those several weeks with some sort of consent from Tess. The phrase "stirred to confused surrender awhile" implies some degree of agency on Tess's part. Far from being purely a victim of others, Tess becomes an active figure complicit in what happens to her and marked with the same moral vulnerability given to each of us. The implication is that we as readers cannot idealize Tess as a creature of perfect innocence. Hardy's description of the affair emphasizes her relative innocence but nevertheless reveals that her participation was not always unwilling.

Tess does not explicitly denounce D'Urberville's unprincipled conduct. She does not criticize his lasciviousness or mount a full argument against the sexual double standard being applied to her. Her closest approach to directly evaluating D'Urberville's behavior and sexual assumptions occurs when she exclaims, in reference to her protestations of innocence, "Did it ever strike your mind that what every woman says some women may feel!"

Tess has left Trantridge after she discovered that her recent behavior goes against her principles; she has "woken up" from her attachment to D'Urberville. Tess cannot share in the world's sexual hypocrisy and will not partake of the arrangements by which men and women trick each other into marriage. Tess is too honest and takes marriage too seriously to be like many other women who get married only to avoid scandal. When Joan says any woman would use the affair as a pretext to force a marriage, Tess replies with simple dignity, "Perhaps any woman would except me." The singularity of Tess's behavior, her reliance on her conscience, and not the customs of society as a guide for authentic behavior, is constantly stressed by Hardy.

Readers of Thomas Hardy's novels have long noted the great care with which Hardy develops detailed accounts of natural landscapes. The importance of the many descriptions of landscape and Nature in Tess is always psychological. The landscape Tess is placed in is immediately revealing of her mental state: the less hospitable the environment, the more negative her psychological condition. Landscape appears as a symbolic reflection of Tess's state of mind.

The psychological treatment of landscape becomes clear near the end of Chapter 13. Hardy discusses Tess's wish to isolate herself, to lose herself in her natural environment, and her feeling that she is wronging that environment through her guilt. Tess goes so far as to interpret natural phenomena as if they were in fact a commentary on her past behavior: "At times her whimsical fancy would intensify natural processes around her till they seemed a part of her own story. Rather they became a part of it; for the world is only a psychological phenomenon, and they seemed they were. The midnight airs and gusts, moaning amongst the tightly-wrapped buds and bark of the winter twigs, were formulae of bitter reproach. A wet day was the expression of irremediable grief..." Readers should note that "the world is only a psychological phenomenon" not just here to Tess, who interprets nature as an extension and reflection of her own mood, but throughout the novel in its descriptions of natural environments.

Tess finally realizes that "The past was past; whatever it had been it was no more at hand." Tess does not succumb to her poverty, her experiences, her guilt, her ostracization. She is not "demoralized." She assimilates her experience and finds a way to re-enter life, to put the past behind her. Throughout this passage of maturity, Hardy indicates the respect he holds for the heroine he has created by describing her beauty, her dignity, and her seriousness. Her voice takes on a note of tragedy, her eyes become more eloquently expressive, her soul is deepened. She realizes that there is more life to be lived. A spirit of "unexpended youth" has not been permanently stilled by her sufferings, and the "invincible instinct towards self-delight" given to all creatures draws Tess out of her isolation and self-punishment and into further engagement with the world.

Interestingly, references to death dot this Phase. Tess is so depressed "she could have hidden herself in a tomb." She tells D'Urberville she would rather not have been born. The hellfire-and-brimstone messages of the sign painter turn on the concepts of death and damnation. The death of Sorrow occupies much of this Phase, and the baptism and burial are set at night, in contrast to the reaping scene, which is preceded by a description of the warm, life-giving sun. While absent-mindedly enduring a winter of empty days, Tess wonders which will be the day of her death, and muses that the date will in the future be unexceptional even to those who knew her. These thoughts prompt Hardy's statement "Almost at a leap Tess thus changed from simple girl to complex woman." A small part of her attraction to going to Talbothays is that the dairy is not far from the family vaults of Tess's D'Urberville ancestors, and thus she will be able to compare her own "lapse" to theirs. Taken together, these references suggest a strong association, if not an affinity, between Tess and death. Hardy is choosing to prepare his readers for later events. Additionally, some readers may wonder that Tess's morbidity and passivity might indicate a self-destructive personality. Why does Tess not fight harder against her fate? Is her ultimate preference not to fight, not to live?

Study Questions

1. Why does Alec want to catch up with and talk to Tess?
2. What final piece of advice does Alec give Tess?
3. Who has started the sign-painter on his work?
4. Why is Tess so struck by the sign-painter's messages?
5. Why is Joan disappointed with Tess?
6. What happens when Tess decides to attend church?
7. What does Tess do after the parson is not allowed in to see her dying infant?
8. What is Tess's reaction to the parson saying her infant may not be allowed a standard Christian burial?
9. What name does Tess give to her infant?
10. Why does Tess wish to leave Marlott?

Answers

1. If he cannot convince her to return to Trantridge, he will at least ride her the rest of the way home to Marlott.
2. Alec advises Tess to display her beauty, her prime advantage, to the world.
3. An evangelical preacher named Mr. Clare started the sign-painter on his unusual work.
4. Tess has the uncanny, irrational feeling that this man knows what has just happened to her.

5. Having heard about Tess being a favorite of Alec, Joan assumes a marriage, which will materially help the Durbeyfields, is in the near future. Joan is shocked and disappointed when she learns otherwise.

6. Her neighbors gossip and whisper in her direction, making Tess feel she is being singled out as one who is guilty.

7. Tess performs the baptism on her own, getting her siblings to pray and reading the prayers herself.

8. Tess vows never to go to the parson's church again.

9. After recollecting a phrase from the book of Genesis in the Bible (Chapter 3, Verse 16: "in sorrow thou shalt bring forth children"), Tess gives her infant the name "Sorrow."

10. Tess feels she cannot be happy in a place which knows the particulars of her lost maidenhood. It is best for her and her family if she moves elsewhere.

Suggested Essay Topics

1. Hardy presents two characters associated with organized religion. What criticisms does he make of these characters and of their religion?

2. Trace and analyze the references to death in this Phase. What does Hardy mean to suggest through these references?

3. How do the landscapes presented in the end of Chapter 13 and throughout Chapter 14 reflect Tess's state of mind? Discuss the details through which Hardy builds informative, and psychologically appropriate portraits of these natural and agricultural environments.

Phase the Third: The Rally
Chapters 16–19

New Characters:

Dairyman Crick: *the kindly and welcoming manager of Talbothays Dairy*

Angel Clare: *a 26-year-old looking for a direction in life*

Reverend Clare: *an earnest, traditional minister scandalized by his son's freethinking nature*

Summary

On a "thyme-scented" May morning, Tess leaves her home for the second time. She is sorry to depart, but she knows her younger siblings will fare better without the presence of their immoral sister.

She travels to the Valley of the Great Dairies, towards Talbothays Dairy. She mentally compares this valley to her native Vale of Blackmoor and notes the immense scale and natural beauty of her destination: "The world was drawn to a larger pattern here...the new air was clear, bracing, ethereal." The main river in the valley of her new home is "as clear as the pure River of Life shown to the Evangelist." Tess begins to feel hope for the future, and is inspired by the "universal...tendency to find sweet pleasure somewhere." She is going to live through her humiliation at the hands of D'Urberville.

Tess meets the master-dairyman of Talbothays, Richard Crick, more commonly known as Dairyman Crick. He greets her warmly, and Tess immediately sets to work milking a cow. Getting to work makes her feel she is laying a new foundation for her future.

The dairyworkers listen to a humorous story from Dairyman Crick. From behind a cow, a male voice utters a rather high-toned reaction. When Tess sees the speaker, she remembers with a start that this was the same man who walked away from the Marlott club-dance without dancing with her. Tess fears to be recognized by this man, but he does not remember her. When she asks her fellow milk-maids who he is, they tell her the man is Angel Clare, a parson's son here to become a gentleman farmer. He is, they say, an intellectual "too much taken up wi' his own thoughts to notice girls."

Angel Clare found his way to Talbothays via a roundabout and unlikely route. His father, the Reverend Clare, is a well-known Evangelical minister who assumes his son Angel will go to Cambridge University prior to a career in the Church of England. Angel, however, has been struck by doubts about his father's religion. Angel scandalizes his father by ordering a book about religious reform.

In the ensuing argument, Angel reveals that he does not believe in one of the primary Articles of Religion of the Church of England and that he has doubts about much of this religion, thus disqualifying him from religious service. To the father, it has always been a family tradition that Cambridge is a "stepping-stone to Orders alone." Angel and his father agree Angel will not go to Cambridge, but will attempt a different path in life.

Angel drifts through several desultory years, marked by development of unorthodox opinions and a brief affair with an older woman in London, until he decides he will become a gentleman farmer. To prepare himself for this career, he is undertaking a series of residencies at different farms to learn all aspects of agriculture. Presently, he finds himself at Talbothays. The effects of this natural, friendly environment on him are beneficial. Surrounded by people of an unfamiliar class, he becomes impressed by the realization of their humanity and individuality; he sees them as people of real worth, instead of looking down on them as mere farm workers. He loses his melancholy and makes a new acquaintance with the world around him.

Angel does not notice Tess until a few days after her arrival. When she asserts that "I do know that our souls can be made to go outside our bodies when we are alive," Angel's ears perk up and he remarks to himself, "What a fresh and virginal daughter of Nature that milkmaid is!" He is sure he has seen this woman before, perhaps on a countryside walk, but can't remember where. The coincidence lodges Tess in his mind, in preference to the dairy's other pretty milkmaids.

After several days, Tess notices that the cows are being arranged so that she can milk the ones who most like her. The author of this favor is Angel Clare. On a June evening, Tess drifts through the outskirts of a garden and hears the notes of a harp played by Clare. They talk, and Tess admits to fears about "life in general." When Angel asks her why she feels this way, Tess describes a dread of the future, a deep conviction that the world is fierce, cruel, and unconsoling. Angel is surprised that this young, wholesome milkmaid is expressing the feelings of her age, "the ache of modernism."

Inevitably, Tess and Angel see more of each other, and each gradually becomes more interested in the other. Tess feels her lack of learning relative to Clare. Angel volunteers to teach Tess about history, but she says she does not want to know that she is just like thousands of people who came before her and thousands who will come after. Tess wonders if her D'Urberville lineage will make Clare, as a student of history, more impressed by her. From Dairyman Crick, though, she learns that Angel believes that old families probably ran through all their usefulness in past days and are now good for nothing.

Analysis

Tess's newfound optimism is supported by the onset of spring and the new life it returns to the world. She leaves on a thyme-scented May morning, emblematic of the spring's regenerative powers. Tess herself is part of this Nature: she felt akin to the landscape. As a part of Nature, Tess partakes of its redemptive powers, its rhythms of growth and transfiguration. "The irresistible, universal, automatic tendency to find sweet pleasure somewhere, which pervades all life, from the meanest to the highest, had at last mastered Tess. Being even now only a young woman of twenty, one who mentally and sentimentally had not finished growing, it was impossible that any event should have left upon her an impression that was not in time capable of transmutation." Growth, change, the will to joy are ever-present forces in Nature and in Tess.

The first half of Chapter 18 focuses exclusively on the background of Angel Clare. For an atypical few pages, Tess drops out of sight. The contrast between Hardy's introduction of Angel and that of Alec, about whose past we are told very little, makes clear that Angel is the second-most important character in the book. We are meant to consider seriously his personality, his struggles, and his potential as a person.

Affected by the contemporary spirit of rationalism, Angel is unable to believe in the literal truth of Jesus' Resurrection and Last Judgment as stated in Article Four of the Articles of Religion: "Christ did truly rise again from death, and took again his body, with flesh, bones, and all things...of Man's nature; wherewith he ascended into Heaven...until he return to judge all Men at the last day." (To be ordained in the Church of England, one must profess belief in all the Articles. Entering Cambridge also required one to swear by the

Articles; most who graduated the school went on to be ordained.) Angel criticizes the Church for propounding an "untenable redemptive theolatry," a phrase implying skepticism about the entire scheme in which God sent His Son to Earth to rescue humans from their sinful natures. His father believes in the glory of God; Angel believes in the glory of man. Reverend Clare stresses the duty man owes to God; Angel stresses the duty man owes to his fellow man.

Hardy uses the contrast between Reverend Clare and Angel to represent the Victorian debate over religion versus morality. Hardy here endorses Angel's opinion, which was the progressive, liberal side of that contemporary social debate.

Angel feels that his father's religion contains things worth preserving and others worth abandoning, and it must therefore be flawed. Reverend Clare feels sending Angel to Cambridge would be a waste if his son did not pursue a religious career. They agree Angel will not attend university. Angel spends some years drifting in search of a suitable vocation. He acquires newfangled opinions. Hardy casually refers to an affair Angel had in London, one he was lucky to get out of without being forced into marriage.

The relationship of Tess and Angel builds very slowly; it takes Angel some time to notice that Tess is there at all. Hardy drops in a comment about Angel's imperceptiveness: "he was ever in the habit of neglecting the particulars of an outward scene for the general impression." Angel's perception, then, sometimes does not do justice to what he is seeing.

Angel first notices Tess when she talks about being able to separate her soul from her body at will. This theological trick arouses Angel's interest, since it echoes on an experiential level a naturalistic alternative to the hidebound religious practice Angel has set aside in his search for higher truth. Angel's first complete thought about her is, "What a fresh and virginal daughter of Nature that milkmaid is!" He interprets her only in terms of the good looks and rustic innocence she outwardly presents. He presumes that since she seems like an innocent country girl she must be a virgin. He believes that the closeness to Nature common to the landworking classes completely defines Tess's personality. These inaccurate presumptions are of lasting importance to Angel's reaction to future events.

Angel discovers that Tess holds some of the same basic convictions of the seriousness and difficulty of life and the doubtful consolations of religion that he does. Their conversation about Tess's "indoor fears," unspecific, existential anxieties about "life in general," makes Angel intrigued by this woman, who articulates thoughts resembling the advanced ideas of the age. Tess feels, through her experience, the "ache of modernism," the dilemma of having nothing to believe in, the feeling of having been thrown into a threatening, unsure world. Angel has, in intellectual fashion, reached the conclusion that the world affords no reliable sources of ultimate value. In time-honored fashion, Tess and Angel start to fall in love because they have similar ideas and philosophies about the world: "something in common" as we might now put it. Although he is intrigued and attracted by Tess, Angel cannot fully perceive that anything truly serious could have happened to a woman he regards as a charmingly unsophisticated country girl.

Study Questions

1. What distinguishes the Valley of the Great Dairies from Blackmoor Vale, where Tess was raised?

2. What is the relationship between Tess's inner mood and her outward beauty?

3. What are Tess's feelings after getting to work milking the cows?

4. Why does Angel Clare reject a career in the Church?

5. What effect does this rejection have on his family's plans for his future?

6. Does Angel notice Tess at first?

7. What comes to Angel's mind after he first pays attention to Tess's presence?

8. How does Angel's time at Talbothays change his attitude towards country folk and his overall mood?

9. What rule of the dairy does Angel break for Tess's benefit?

10. What does Angel think about aristocratic families, according to Dairyman Crick?

Answers

1. The Valley of the Great Dairies is larger than, and perhaps not so beautiful as, the valley in which Tess has so far lived her life.

2. There is an inverse relationship: when her mood is less happy, her beauty is greater; when she is happy, her looks are more or less ordinary.

3. Getting to work gives Tess a sense of security and confidence. She "appeared to feel that she really had laid a new foundation for her future."

4. Affected by the contemporary spirit of rationalism, Angel is unable to believe in the literal truth of Jesus' Resurrection and Last Judgment as stated in Article Four of the Articles of Religion. Angel concludes that since he does not believe all of this religion he cannot rightly take orders in it.

5. The Reverend Clare feels that to send Angel to Cambridge for an education would be a waste if he did not use that education as training for a religious career. Thus, Angel and he agree Angel will not attend Cambridge. Angel spends some years drifting in search of a suitable vocation.

6. Angel does not notice Tess until several days after her arrival at Talbothays.

7. Angel is struck by the vague thought that he has seen her somewhere before. He says to himself, "What a fresh and virginal daughter of Nature that milkmaid is!"

8. Living with farm workers, Angel begins to see them as individual people rather than as stereotypical country bumpkins. He becomes less melancholy as he spends more time outdoors.

9. Angel lines up the cows so that Tess will be able to milk her favorites.

10. Dairyman Crick tells Tess that the strongest of Angel's unorthodox opinions is a hatred of old, aristocratic families, whom Angel feels have used their best energies and seen their best days in the past.

Suggested Essay Topics

1. Research the Victorian reaction against organized religion, especially as embodied in the Articles of Faith of the Church of England. How typical were Angel Clare's misgivings about religion and religious faith?

2. Hardy writes of Angel, "[H]e made close acquaintance with phenomena which he had before known but darkly—the seasons in their moods, morning and evening, night and noon, winds in their different tempers, trees, waters, and mists, shades and silence, and the voices of inanimate things." Citing and analyzing several passages descriptive of nature, argue that this quotation names those things Hardy most wants us to perceive and appreciate as we read the novel.

3. How does Angel misjudge and misperceive Tess even as he first begins to be attracted to her?

Phase the Third: The Rally
Chapters 20–24

New Characters:

Retty Priddle: *a young milkmaid, fair and auburn-haired, in love with Angel Clare*

Izz Huett: *a pale, dark-haired milkmaid, in love with Angel Clare*

Marian: *the oldest of the three milkmaids in love with Angel Clare*

Summary

Under the influence of the warm summer sun and a natural world teeming with the sights and juices of regeneration and fertilization, the attraction between Tess Durbeyfield and Angel Clare continues to grow. Possibly by chance, the two are the first up each day at the dairy, and they view each other in the "aqueous" light of dawn. Tess appears nearly a goddess of feminine beauty, a "divinity." Clare's appreciation for her increases; inspired by her awesome and rare beauty, Angel teasingly, affectionately calls her by the names of ancient Greek goddesses, such as Artemis and Demeter.

Not understanding these references, Tess asks to be called by her true name. Tess is depressed when she realizes she is much less educated than Angel.

One day a minor crisis hits the dairy. The churn will not produce any butter. Dairyman Crick recalls a previous time when the butter would not come; this happened because a man named Jack Dollop was inside the churn, hiding from an angry mother who claimed he had stolen the honor of her daughter. The story provides a good laugh to all but Tess, who sees in it a reflection of her own shameful past. Tess runs outside, where the sky looks to her like an inflamed wound.

Tess's fellow milkmaids, Izz Huett, Retty Priddle, and Marian, meanwhile, all admit to an infatuation with Angel Clare. They know their love for him is hopeless, both because he is out of their class, and because they are sure that Tess is his favorite. While Tess knows she is more attractive as a woman and potential wife than her friends, she has vowed to herself never to marry.

Another crisis mobilizes the farmfolk: the butter just made at the dairy is bitter. Dairyman Crick figures it must be due to some garlic in a field where the cows have been grazing. Angel manages to work alongside Tess, and they get a chance to talk. Tess, fighting against her own attraction to Clare, commends the feminine charms of her fellow milkmaids in preference to her own; but her heart is not fully in this evasion, because she feels herself more and more drawn to this dutiful young man. Tess is moved to respect Angel because he acts so conscientiously toward the milkmaids infatuated with him. To Tess, such respectful behavior is unique among the men she has known.

A few Sundays later, Tess, Izz, Retty, and Marian walk to Mellstock for church. Angel, who prefers sermons in stones to those in church, is out in the fields. The milkmaids, dressed in their Sunday best, are checked by a flooded lane. Angel sees the women, and volunteers to carry each of them across. For the panting, lovestruck women, to be so close to their beloved Clare is an agonizing pleasure. The last to be carried across is Tess: "Three Leahs to get one Rachel!" says Angel, referring to the Bible story in which Jacob must endure seven years of marriage to Leah before being allowed to marry his true love Rachel. The incident forces Tess to

admit that there was "no concealing from herself the fact that she loved Angel Clare."

One day, Angel and Tess work near each other in an isolated part of the dairy. Tess's aesthetic power, her concord with the natural world's beauty, and her tremendous, singular lips move Angel, perhaps against his rational judgment, to leap up and embrace his beloved. Tess instinctively but briefly yields to the embrace of her lover before she pushes him away because her cow may be upset by this unusual sight. Clare avows his love for Tess. The horizons of these two lives will be forever altered.

Analysis

Phase the Third contains the most extended pictorial descriptions in the novel, as well as some of the most beautiful, poetic, evocative prose Hardy ever wrote. Throughout these chapters, Hardy correlates the minds and hearts of his characters with the warm, passionate, fertile, natural world they inhabit. The sensuous atmosphere at Talbothays is evoked through descriptions of the season and environment—Hardy's portraits of the landscape communicate the conditions governing this phase of Tess's life. "Rays from the sunrise drew forth the buds and stretched them into long stalks, lifted up sap in noiseless streams, opened petals, and sucked out scents in invisible jets and breathings." In an environment so rife with "germination," it is inevitable that Tess and Angel are "converging, under an irresistible law, as surely as two streams in one vale." Hardy underlines the connection between nature and human behavior: "Amid the oozing fatness and warm ferments of the Var Vale, at a season when the rush of juices could almost be heard below the hiss of fertilization, it was impossible that the most fanciful love should not grow passionate. The ready bosoms existing there were impregnated by their surroundings." Tess, being a pure and natural woman, feels suited to this environment, and is happier here than she has ever been.

Hardy's metaphors in Chapter 20, in which Angel and Tess court in the aqueous light of dawn, are extraordinarily thorough and beautiful. Tess's transcendent beauty is communicated through natural metaphors. She herself, says Hardy, lights up the environment as if by phosphorescence. Tess is connected to

Nature, part of its entirety, linked to the birds flying through the morning fog. "Birds would soar through [the fog] into the upper radiance, and hang on the wing sunning themselves, or alight on the wet rails subdividing the mead, which now shone like glass rods…diamonds of moisture from the mist hung, too, upon Tess's eyelashes, and drops upon her hair, like seed pearls." Tess is completely unalienated from Nature. Hardy's language becomes poetic: its use of finely observed details and its implicit association between Tess and the environment point to Hardy's later career as a poet.

Given the extraordinary vision Tess presents, Angel Clare can scarcely be blamed for idealizing her. To the sensitive and intellectual Clare, Tess is reminiscent of mythical figures of womanhood. She encapsulates the attractions of the entire opposite sex. Hardy tracks Angel's thoughts carefully here: "She was no longer the milkmaid, but a visionary essence of woman—a whole sex condensed into one typical form. He called her Artemis, Demeter, and other fanciful names half teasingly, which she did not like because she did not understand them." Tess fears such adoration and simply wants to be seen for who she is. Call me Tess, she says, and so Angel does.

Knowing she plans not to marry, Tess, in self-negating and self-protective fashion, tries to turn Angel's attentions to the other milkmaids, her friends Izz Huett, Retty Priddle, and Marian. Hardy presents another aspect of romantic love through these characters, who as a group illustrate the direct connections in Hardy's mind between women, love, and Nature. "The air of the sleeping-chamber seemed to palpitate with the hopeless passion of the girls. They writhed feverishly under the oppressiveness of an emotion thrust on them by cruel Nature's law—an emotion which they had neither expected nor desired….The differences which distinguished them as individuals were abstracted by this passion, and each was but portion of one organism called sex." Their love is pure, involuntary, and so egoless that it makes the milkmaids seem not individuals but only a part of their sex (or gender). Their love contains no thoughts about consequences (class differences make a marriage unlikely), and thus no anxious calculations about the future. Nature, a blind and undiscriminating

force, causes these women to experience love. As natural beings, the milkmaids inevitably are attracted to Angel. He is an acceptable man, and they, as women, must desire such a man. The impulse to love, Hardy shows, comes from outside our conscious selves.

In Chapter 24, Hardy describes the lovers' first embrace in passionate terms, but he also makes clear that Angel is a creature of impulse, somewhat taken aback by his own actions. By shading celebration with qualification, Hardy gently hints that the love of Angel for Tess will not be a case of happily ever after.

Study Questions

1. Who are usually the first two people to wake each day at Talbothays?

2. What names does Angel call Tess?

3. What is responsible for the Talbothays butter having a bitter "twang"?

4. What is Tess's opinion of herself as a woman as compared to the other milkmaids?

5. Who carries Tess, Marian, Izz, and Retty across a flooded lane?

6. What quality exhibited by Angel earns him Tess's respect?

7. How do the milkmaids react when they surmise Angel's affections are only for Tess, and why have the milkmaids thought it unlikely Angel would consider them as future wives?

8. Whom is Angel supposed to marry?

9. What technique does Tess use in milking cows?

10. What part of Tess's body is deemed by Angel to be the most enticing?

Answers

1. Angel and Tess, "possibly not always by chance," are the first two people to arise each day at the dairy-house.

2. Angel calls her Artemis and Demeter, the names of women from Greek mythology. Artemis was the virgin goddess of the hunt; Demeter was the goddess of fertility.

3. A few garlic shoots in a nearby meadow are responsible for imparting a bitter flavor to the butter recently produced at Talbothays. The last time this happened, Dairyman Crick thought the meadow was "bewitched"; now he has arrived at a more plausible hypothesis.

4. Tess realizes that she is "more finely formed, better educated...and more woman than" any of her friends.

5. Angel carries the milkmaids across a flooded lane as they attempt to make their way to church.

6. Tess is impressed by Clare's sense of self-control and duty in not taking advantage of Retty's, Marian's, and Izz's attraction to him.

7. The milkmaids' attitudes are largely of fatalistic resignation. They do not envy Tess because they accept the fact they never had any real chance of permanently attracting Clare's attentions. The milkmaids assume they have no chance with Angel because he is from a different class.

8. The milkmaids have heard that his parents want Angel to marry a woman of his own class, who is a daughter of a Doctor of Divinity.

9. Tess, like the younger milkmaids, tends to rest her head sideways on the cow, looking out into the distance.

10. It is her mouth that exemplifies Tess's physical beauty to Angel. "[H]er mouth he had seen nothing to equal on the face of the earth. To a young man with the least fire in him that little upward lift in the middle of her red top lip was distracting, infatuating, maddening."

Suggested Essay Topics

1. Trace the connections Hardy suggests between the natural environment at Talbothays, the summer season, and the growing love of Angel and Tess.

2. Analyze Hardy's language in this passage: "The air of the sleeping-chamber seemed to palpitate with the hopeless passion of the girls. They writhed feverishly under the op- pressiveness of an emotion thrust on them by cruel Nature's law—an emotion which they had neither expected nor desired....The differences which distinguished them as in- dividuals were abstracted by this passion, and each was but portion of one organism called sex." What connections is Hardy assuming between women and emotionality, and be- tween women and Nature? How could you use this passage to argue that Hardy's view of Nature is not straightforwardly positive but rather complex and ambiguous?

Phase the Fourth: The Consequence
Chapters 25–29

New Characters:

Reverend Felix Clare: *Angel's brother, a curate*

Reverend Cuthbert Clare: *Angel's brother, a classical scholar and fellow and dean of his college at Cambridge*

Mrs. Clare: *the second wife of Reverend Clare, a good-hearted, sympathetic, but slightly snobbish, woman*

Beck Knibbs: *a wife who believes in withholding information from husbands and smacking them if they don't like it*

Mercy Chant: *a devout and well-brought-up young girl whom Angel's parents have selected as his future wife*

Summary

Hours after their embrace, Tess feels "stilled, almost alarmed." Angel guiltily believes that his "feeling had won the better of judg- ment." As a man of conscience, Angel realizes that Tess's future fortunes in life are his responsibility, something he must treat as seriously as he does his own life. Feeling he should not take ad- vantage of the situation by being in such close proximity to Tess, he makes an impromptu visit to his family at Emminster Vicarage. The visit makes the milkmaids ask when Angel will be leaving permanently; they agonize over the news that he has about four months left at Talbothays before moving on to another farm.

At Emminster, Angel is warmly greeted by his father and mother, as well as his older brothers. Felix is a curate in a nearby town, and Cuthbert is a classical scholar at Cambridge. His family notes a change in Clare: he is more countrified, carrying himself less like a scholar or drawing-room gentleman. His time away from home has led Angel to contemplate the limitations of his brothers. They are willing followers of intellectual trends who have isolated themselves within their occupational circles. "Felix seemed to him all Church; Cuthbert all College." His father is the most rigidly earnest of all his family, but seems to Angel to have a warmer heart than either of his brothers. In fact, his father has set aside money for Angel to buy farmland.

After a meal, Angel broaches the subject he has come to discuss, the possibility of marriage to Tess. His parents wish for Angel a "truly Christian woman," and urge Mercy Chant, an exceptionally devout woman who is the daughter of a friend, upon Clare. Angel says he is instead thinking of a woman who would be a helpmate in his agricultural career. Although his mother, carrying middle-class prejudices against the lower rungs of society, is disappointed that Angel's intended is not a "lady," both parents are glad when Angel discusses Tess's religious orthodoxy and her frequent churchgoing. They tell Angel not to act hurriedly but that they will consent to meet his choice.

On the way out of town, Reverend Clare walks with Angel and tells his son about a young reprobate by the name of D'Urberville that he tried unsuccessfully to reform. Angel worries that preaching so directly to the unregenerate places his father in physical risk.

Returning to Talbothays in the early afternoon, Angel's mood is affected as if he has thrown off splints and bandages. All but Tess are away or taking naps; Tess herself is just arising. He embraces her again, saying he has come back early on her account, while "Tess's excitable heart beat against his by way of reply." Working together skimming the milk, Angel proposes to Tess, perhaps "without quite meaning himself to do it so soon." Tess says she cannot marry Angel,

although she loves him and is engaged to no one else. Asked why she nevertheless refuses, Tess invents the excuse that she is not high-born enough to suit his parents. To move the conversation to a less stressful topic, Clare tells his father's story about trying to reform Alec D'Urberville. When Angel asks again about marriage, Tess, with that name ringing in her ears, cries out, "It can't be!"

Feeling that Tess, like other women, is saying no only to say yes later, Angel continues to woo Tess. When Tess says she declines because she is not "worthy," Angel assumes she is talking about not being a refined lady. He praises her mental versatility; in fact, Tess has already begun to pick up some of Angel's intellectual and conversational habits.

Drawn together by the chore of crumbling the curd, Angel seizes the chance of kissing Tess's arm and is rewarded by a de-voted smile from his beloved. Angel proposes again. In reply, Tess says she will tell him all about herself and her experiences on Sun-day. Her conscience tells her these experiences will make any mar-riage, especially one to a respectable man, a misery. But she knows the force of her love for Angel is making acquiescence inevitable. "I shall let myself marry him—I cannot help it!" she cries out.

On Sunday, Dairyman Crick recounts another episode in the life of ne'er-do-well Jack Dollop. Dollop married a widow because she had an annual income of 50 pounds, only to find the income ceased upon her remarriage. The dairy-workers laugh at the story and argue about whether the widow should have told the truth about her situation prior to the marriage. A consensus opinion is from Beck Knibbs: "If he'd said two words to me about not telling him beforehand...I'd ha' knocked him down wi' the rolling pin." To the workers, the story is a comedy; to Tess, it is a tragedy.

Angel again asks Tess to marry him; she refuses, for his sake, but she knows her moral scruples cannot continue to hold forth against her passionate love for Clare. One evening after the skim-ming, Dairyman Crick needs someone to ride some milk to the train station; Clare volunteers and asks Tess to go along.

Analysis

Hardy reveals crucial information about Angel Clare by con-trasting him to the rest of his family. Clare's brothers are creatures of intellectual conventionality; they are secure in their careers, as Angel is not, but they are severely limited, willfully ignoring life outside their social and intellectual circles. That Angel seeks a different path than his "hallmarked" brothers indicates his freethinking skepticism is a sincere and genuine trait, of which Hardy approves.

We see that Angel does not want his choice of a wife to disappoint his parents. This admirable impulse, however, leads him to emphasize qualities in Tess that are not the ones that drew her to him. Thus, he exaggerates Tess's churchgoing and her common piety, which are things that at Talbothays do not count to Angel for very much. Within the orbit of his parents, Angel comes to see Tess as a sort of project; if she is taught religion and given cultivation by Angel, she will be acceptable to his parents. Tess, in fact, is an able student. She once did well in school and wanted to become a teacher. "Her natural quickness, and her admiration for him, having led her to pick up his vocabulary, his accent, and fragments of his knowledge, to a surprising extent." Despite her abilities, however, we experience a slight unease: why does Angel feel a need to embellish Tess's personality?

Tess's life continues to be plagued by ironic coincidence, or, to put it another way, bad timing. Whenever events take an optimistic turn, a chance occurrence suddenly checks her attainment of happiness. Clare thinks he is changing the conversation to a more neutral topic in bringing up Alec D'Urberville, but, unbeknownst to him, he has just named the person whose existence is Tess's reason for refusing Clare. When Tess goes outside after the story about Jack Dollop, Angel follows her, takes her by the waist, and asks her again to marry him. So shocked is he by Tess's emphatic "no," uttered in momentary overreaction to this laughable story, that he lets her go and does not attempt the kiss. "It all turned on that release," notes the narrator. If Angel had seized that moment to kiss her, she would have said yes, and their story, Hardy seems to imply, may have had a happy ending.

Inside Tess there is a battle between an urge to tell Clare the truth about herself and a desire to seize the chance at happiness he represents to her. She wishes to "snatch ripe pleasure before the iron teeth of pain could have time to shut upon her." Her conscience, powerful as always, reminds her of two thoughts: that she must make a complete confession of her past to Clare, lest he find out after the marriage and accuse her of deceit, and that her union with D'Urberville has in a religious sense…a certain moral validity. Tess knows her emotional and physical passion for Clare is stronger than these reservations. "Every see-saw of her breath, every wave of her blood, every pulse singing in her ears, was a voice that joined with nature in revolt against her scrupulousness." Tess knows she will submit to her feelings for Clare, whom she sees almost as a god. Her acquiescence is not without an element of pride and possessiveness: "I can't bear to let anybody have him but me!"

Clare plays the part of the persistent lover in fine fashion, and his love for Tess is pure and genuine; "his manner," writes Hardy, "was so much that of one who would love and cherish and defend her under any conditions, changes, or revelations, that her gloom lessened as she basked in it."

Study Questions

1. How long will Angel remain at Talbothays?

2. What gifts from Mrs. Crick does Angel carry home to his family at Emminster?

3. What changes does his family note in Angel?

4. What qualities are the Clares looking for in a future daughter-in-law?

5. Who is Mercy Chant?

6. How much forethought lies behind the timing of Angel's first proposal to Tess?

7. What rationale does Tess use to explain this initial refusal?

8. What story about his father does Angel tell Tess?

9. How does Tess react to the story about the woeful rogue Jack Dollop?

10. On what errand does Tess accompany Clare?

Answers

1. Angel is planning to stay at Talbothays for about four more months before visiting another farm.

2. Angel carries home two gifts from Mrs. Crick to his family: black-pudding and mead (an alcoholic beverage made from fermented honey).

3. Angel seems more countrified, carrying himself more like a farmer and less like the scholar his family had hoped him to be.

4. The Clares want a God-fearing, Christian woman for their son. Mrs. Clare, additionally, is concerned that her son marry a "lady."

5. Mercy Chant is the woman Clare's parents hope and expect he will marry. She is a church-going, devout girl, the daughter of family friends.

6. Angel had not meant to propose so quickly. His proposal is rather impulsive.

7. Tess seizes on the idea (which is, unknown to her, more than partially true) that she is not upper-class or learned enough to fit in with Angel's social circle and his family.

8. To bring the conversation to a more general and less stressful level, Angel tells of a young, dissolute squire named D'Urberville whom his father tried to convert to a more holy life.

9. Tess is horrified that everyone laughs at the story of Jack Dollop, whose future wife did not tell him all about her past history before they got married. Tess feels that the story, which echoes her own dilemma, is quite serious.

10. On a chilly September night, Angel and Tess ride some milk to the railway station, where it will be shipped to London.

Suggested Essay Topics

1. Compare Angel Clare to his brothers. How do their achievements and limitations underline both what is questionable and what is admirable about Angel's character?

2. Does Hardy want us to think well of Angel Clare's parents? (That is, do their good qualities outweigh their bad ones?) Provide evidence on both sides and reach an appropriate conclusion.

3. Secure a copy of Matthew Arnold's *Culture and Anarchy* (first published, 1869). Read Chapter IV for Arnold's account of Hellenism (right-thinking, free play of the mind) versus Hebraism (rightness of conduct, severity of conscience). By the time Hardy wrote *Tess,* these labels were well established in England. Now explain Angel's remark that it might have been better if Greece and not Palestine had served as "the source of the religion of modern civilization." How well does Reverend Clare embody Hebraism and Angel Hellenism?

Phase the Fourth: The Consequence
Chapters 30–34

New Characters:

A man from Trantridge: *recalling Tess's past, he makes a judgmental comment about her*

The carriage driver: *a broken-down, 60-year-old with a running wound on his leg*

Jonathan Kail: *a simple minded farm worker*

Summary

Along the way to the station, Angel points out Wellbridge Manor, a converted farmhouse that was once a mansion belonging to the D'Urberville family. Angel again pleads with Tess to marry him. She says she must first tell him about her history and begins to tell him about her upbringing and hometown. Just as she is about to tell her past troubles, she says instead that she is not a Durbeyfield, but a D'Urberville. Angel takes this for the revelation she was concealing, and Tess does not correct this misimpression. He sees the news of her ancestry as positive, since society, and especially his mother, will be more accepting of Tess if she has noble blood. Tess finally says "Yes!" to Angel, and immediately sobs. She asks for permission to write her mother. When she says she lives in Marlott, Angel finally realizes where he has seen her. Tess hopes that being overlooked that day will not turn out to be an ill omen.

Joan sends a letter to Tess, advising her not to tell Angel about her past problems. Tess feels that the responsibility has been lifted from her shoulders, and she and Clare enjoy open-air courting. Angel asks Tess to fix their marriage date, but Tess is reluctant, preferring a "perpetual betrothal." After they are caught embracing, Angel announces to Crick and their friends at the dairy that they will be married soon. The milkmaids are awestruck at Tess's news. Their admiration activates Tess's guilt: "You are all better than I!" She vows again to tell Clare her past.

Fewer milkmaids are necessary as winter comes, and Angel uses this fact to force Tess's hand. They agree to get married by the end of the year. Angel has an opportunity to work at a flour-mill nearby at that time. Angel decides on Wellbridge Manor, near this flour-mill, as a honeymoon site. The wedding is set for December 31. Angel has taken a wedding license, rather than having the banns of marriage announced in church; he has also asked the Cricks to keep the date a secret. These arrangements please Tess, who desires privacy so that no one will tell Angel about D'Urberville, but she fears she will pay for her good fortune. Angel buys Tess wedding clothes.

To enjoy some time together before the wedding, Angel and Tess go into town for Christmas Eve. While waiting for Angel, Tess is observed by a man from the Trantridge area. This man begins to insult Tess; when Angel hears these words, he punches the man. The stranger apologizes, Angel gives him five pounds, and they part with no hard feelings. That night, Clare acts out the fight in his sleep, and Tess vows to inform him, this time in writing, all about herself. She puts a four-page letter under his door. The next day he shows no response; could she have been forgiven already? The morning of her wedding, she realizes he must not have read the letter. She discovers that it was wedged out of sight, under a carpet near his door. The anxious bridesmaid asks to be allowed to make a confession of her faults. Angel brushes her worries aside, saying they should both be perfect to each other on their wedding day.

The crowd at the church is small. Neither Angel's parents nor brothers nor Tess's parents attend. To Tess, sublimely in love with Clare, nothing matters except her husband. She "felt glorified by an irradiation not her own," so overpowering to her was the joy of wedding Angel.

After the ceremony, Tess becomes downcast, oppressed by a sense of seriousness. Angel attempts to jest her out of this mood, making a quip about the Wellbridge Manor being one of Tess's "ancestral mansions." They are alone at the manor for their first night as a wedded couple, and enjoy a meal together. A messenger arrives with a package for "Mrs. Angel Clare." Inside is a full set of jewels—a gift from Angel's now-deceased godmother, to be given to whomever Angel married. The jewelry accentuates Tess's natural beauty. Jonathan Kail arrives, rather later than expected, with some of their belongings. He was delayed by unhappy events at Talbothays.

Retty Priddle has tried to drown herself; Marian, never a drinker, got dead drunk; and Izz Huett has fallen into a depression. Tess reflects to herself that those with the most reason to be unhappy pretend otherwise, and she vows to tell Angel everything. "She would pay to the uttermost farthing; she would tell, there and then." Angel broaches the subject first, saying he would like to confess something to Tess that he should have told her before. Exactly Tess's situation!

Angel launches into his confession. He is not a wicked person, he says, but he once acted immorally by indulging in "eight-and-forty hours' dissipation with a stranger" in London. Tess forgives Angel. Feeling joyously certain she will be forgiven for the same fault, Tess, in a steady voice, begins the painful narrative of her acquaintance with Alec D'Urberville.

Analysis

Angel's previously expressed ideals about the decline of old families are belied by his joy at the news of Tess's lineage. Her ancestry will make her more acceptable to his family because "society is slightly snobbish." (Clearly, for society we can insert Angel.) Angel will now be able to present Tess "triumphantly" as a lady. Hardy notes sarcastically that, "Perhaps Tess's lineage had more value for himself than for anybody in the world besides."

Tess's reaction when Angel keeps their wedding a relative secret articulates a tragic perspective on life. "I don't feel easy," Tess
says to herself. "All this good fortune may be scourged out of me
afterwards by a lot of ill. That's how Heaven mostly does." Tess articulates the concept of retributive justice: humans will be punished for their pleasure. Tess's thought echoes the Greek idea of
the god Nemesis (or enemy), who strikes at anyone with the pre-
sumption to enjoy too much pride or satisfaction in life.

Tess prefers what Hardy terms a perpetual betrothal rather
than a wedding date fixed in time. Even at her life's greatest period
of happiness, she fears the consequences of marrying Angel, and
is beset by doubt, fear, moodiness, care, and shame. She wishes
that her life could always be just as it is now, "that it would always
be summer and autumn, and you always courting me, always
thinking as much of me as you have always done through the past
summer-time!" The metaphor linking her life to the season underscores Tess's connection to nature.

The power of Tess's conscience is subdued by a passivity and
willlessness that are equally characteristic of this contradictory
heroine. When her mother advises her not to tell Clare about Alec,
Tess feels a burden of responsibility has been lifted from her. When
she discovers Clare has not read her confessional letter, she knows
there is time enough to tell him before the wedding, but chooses
not to do so.

Angel's capacity to love is closely analyzed by Hardy. In order
to make later events credible, and in order to emphasize Tess's victimization by even such as Clare who love her, Hardy continues to
provide explanations for Clare's behavior which we can use to judge
him. He could love desperately, but with a love more inclined to
the imaginative and the ethereal; it was a fastidious emotion, which
could jealously guard the loved one against his very self. Angel, it
is suggested, tends to love not the woman in front of him but an
idealized or spiritualized vision of her; and he may be using his
love to protect himself against certain aspects of his personality.
Note the contrast between Angel's limited, partial love for Tess and
Tess's complete adoration of Angel: "There was hardly a touch of
earth in her love for Clare. To her sublime trustfulness he was all
that goodness could be." She so idolizes Angel that she prays to

him and not to God. Such devotion is surely misplaced, Hardy notes. In her reaction from indignation against the male sex, Tess swerved to excess of honor for Clare.

At the wedding, Angel's partial knowledge of the extent of her love for him is revealed. "Clare knew that she loved him—every curve of her form showed that—but he did not know at that time the full depth of her devotion, its single-mindedness, its meekness; what long suffering it guaranteed, what honesty, what endurance, what good faith." These aspects of love, traditionally thought to be feminine, are precisely what Tess will show in superabundance in the course of future events.

Hardy communicates the unhappy outcome of the marriage by ill omens. The grotesque touch of the carriage-driver with a running wound introduces a jarring note, which is amplified by a reference to the darkly mysterious (but here unexplained) legend of the D'Urberville coach. The crowing of a cock in the afternoon is interpreted as a bad sign for the future.

Hardy again creates a chain of events which entraps poor Tess. When she hears of the dairymaids' unhappy reactions to her marriage, she vows decisively to tell Clare about herself, again using strong language of self-condemnation: "It was wicked of her to take all without paying. She would pay to the uttermost farthing; she would tell, there and then."

The final picture Hardy leaves us with is charged with foreboding. The image relies upon the patterning of red and white that seems to follow Tess throughout her life. "Imagination might have beheld a Last Day luridness in this red-coaled glow [of the fire], which fell on his face and hand, and on hers, peering into the loose hair about her brow, and firing on the delicate skin underneath... She bent forward, at which each diamond on her neck gave a sinister wink like a toad's..." The description is pure pathetic fallacy. What this situation looks like, it feels like.

Study Questions

1. What is Angel's true attitude toward the decline of renowned families?

2. What is the only modern encroachment upon the pastoral area around Talbothays?

3. Why is Angel cheered by Tess's revelation that she is a D'Urberville?

4. What premarital advice does Joan give Tess?

5. Does Angel allow news of the marriage to be publicized?

6. Why is Angel forced to punch the man from Trantridge?

7. Do any of Angel's or Tess's close relatives attend the wedding?

8. What is Tess's mood after the ceremony?

9. How do Marian, Izz, and Retty behave after the ceremony?

10. Where do Angel and Tess go for their honeymoon?

Answers

1. Angel does not believe that noble blood equals individual virtue, but his emotions are stirred by the story of a family come down in the world.

2. A railway line is the only modern intrusion upon the area around Talbothays.

3. He feels that "society is slightly snobbish," and Angel believes Tess's aristocratic lineage will make her more respectable and impressive to his family.

4. Joan counsels Tess not to tell Angel about the relationship with D'Urberville.

5. Angel asks the Cricks to keep the wedding date secret and also asks that the banns (announcements of an upcoming marriage) not be called out in church. He has arranged instead for a marriage license.

6. The man from Trantridge has just stopped himself from completing an insult of Tess. To avenge this attempted slight, Angel punches the man.

7. No one from either Tess's or Angel's immediate family attends the marriage ceremony.

8. After the ceremony, Tess is apprehensive and fearful about the future. Angel tries to coax and joke her out of this mood.

9. In the hours after the wedding, Retty Priddle has tried to drown herself, Marian got very drunk, and Izz Huett has fallen into a severe depression.

10. Angel and Tess go to Wellbridge Manor, a converted farmhouse once owned by the D'Urbervilles.

Suggested Essay Topics

1. Readers have criticized Hardy for inserting too many unlikely coincidences in the plots of his novels. Is the episode of Tess's letter being mistakenly placed under the rug excessively arbitrary or unlikely? If Hardy does depart from the limits of a strict realism here, is it for a valid artistic purpose? Would Tess's tragedy have been prevented if Angel had read the letter?

2. Tess's desire, Hardy states, is not so much to be a wife as it is to live in a state of "perpetual betrothal," eternally promised, but never married to Angel Clare. Is there a feminist insight here about the unworkability of marriage and its basic unfairness to women? To a woman, what are the advantages and disadvantages of a "perpetual betrothal" as compared to a traditional marriage? What other moments in Phase the Fourth show that Hardy is aware of how women suffer in society?

3. Hardy intimates throughout these chapters that the love Angel has for Tess may be insufficient, limited, flawed. How does Hardy suggest the limits to Angel's love, and to his character as a whole, without losing his readers' basic sympathy for and approval of Clare?

4. "Phase the Fourth is the most tragic segment of this novel because it is here that the distance between Tess and happiness seems the shortest." Justify this statement.

5. Trace the influence of the D'Urberville family over the events of these chapters. How does Tess's ancestry recur as a determining factor in her life?

Phase the Fifth: The Woman Pays
Chapters 35–44

Summary

Angel simply cannot think after Tess's revelation. Tess pleads to be forgiven as she has forgiven Angel, but to Angel it is as if he is looking at another woman in the shape of Tess. The pair wander the countryside at night, Tess walking behind Clare. Tess even volunteers to kill herself, but Angel will not allow such an absurd action. When they get home, Tess goes into their bedroom and eventually falls asleep. Clare is about to enter the room when he is checked by the sight of the merciless, arrogant portraits of Tess's D'Urberville ancestors, which bear a resemblance to her.

For several days, the newlyweds lead a formal existence. Angel demands to know if her story is true; Tess sadly says yes. Clare asks if the man in question is still living, and again Tess replies yes. Angel vents angry sarcasm at the thought that he rejected a socially advantageous marriage yet has, nevertheless, been deprived of the rustic innocence he thought Tess represented. Tess points out that "it is in your own mind what you are angry at...it is not in me."

Angel cannot accept that their marriage is authentic, since D'Urberville and not he is Tess's "husband in Nature." Even if he could accept their marriage, their children, he points out, would bear calumny if the true history of their mother were revealed. Perhaps if the man were dead, that would make a difference, Angel tells her. Tess suggests divorce, but Angel does not consider it an option because of his religion. Never arguing for herself, Tess meekly takes Angel's rejection and coldness as her due. She is willing to do whatever Angel commands. After several days, they discuss parting. Angel recommends the idea, telling Tess, "I think of people more kindly when I am away from them."

The night before they are to part, Angel sleepwalks, carrying Tess across a narrow footbridge and then laying her down in an empty stone coffin. In his sleep, Angel cries out "Dead! Dead! Dead!" but also admits his love for Tess. The next morning, he shows no recollection, and she decides not to mention the incident. Husband and wife separate: Tess will journey back home to her family

at Marlott. Angel places 50 pounds and the wedding jewels in trust to provide Tess spending money. "Until I come to you," he says, "it is better that you should not try to come to me."

At home, Tess tells her mother her husband is not with her, but she covers up the true extent of the split. When Tess tearfully says she confessed her past to her husband, Joan ridicules her for not taking her advice. When John Durbeyfield is told his daughter has returned home, he asks, "D'ye think he really have married her?—or is it like the first?" Not being trusted by her own father is a blow to Tess's pride. Seeing there is no room in the house for her, and feeling that she brings discredit upon her family, Tess leaves, giving 25 pounds to her family to compensate for the suffering she has put them through.

Clare's troubles cannot be lessened by the consoling philosophy he has learned. He visits his parents, telling them when they are surprised by his wife's absence, that he is going alone to Brazil for a year to investigate farming opportunities, and his parents will meet his bride later on. Sensing trouble, Mrs. Clare asks Angel if his wife is the sort of woman "whose history bears investigation." Angel lies, saying Tess is "spotless." At dinner, his father reads from the Bible King Lemuel's praise of a good wife: "Who can find a virtuous woman? for her price is far above rubies." A "slave to custom and conventionality when surprised back into his early teachings," Angel cannot perceive that Tess deserves such praise as much as any other woman.

Angel must go to Wellbridge Manor, the site of his honeymoon, to pick up a few belongings. On the road he sees Izz Huett. Feeling he has been treated unfairly and been too respectful of convention, Angel asks Izz to accompany him to Brazil. When he asks if Izz loves him more than Tess does, she truthfully answers that no one could love Angel more than Tess: "She would have laid down her life for 'ee. I could do no more!" A chastened Angel urges Izz to forget the invitation.

Through the spring, summer, and early fall, Tess supports herself doing light farm work, not touching the money Angel gave her. After harvest-time she is in straitened circumstances and must spend some of the money. She clings to the hope that Angel will soon return from Brazil to join her. Unbeknownst to her, Angel lies in Brazil sick from fever. Disdaining indoor work, Tess makes her way toward an upland farm where her friend Marian works. On the way, Tess encounters the Trantridge man who tried to insult her before her marriage, and she runs away from him into a forest. There she sleeps on a bed of dry leaves. She hears strange noises, and at dawn realizes she is surrounded by dying pheasants who have been shot down by hunters. Ashamed that she thought her own misery greater than the sufferings of the wounded birds, Tess mercifully snaps the necks of the doomed pheasants.

The next day Tess reaches the farm at Flintcomb-Ash, a desolate, featureless, cold, barren place. Tess is given a position doing the roughest kind of farm work. Marian is surprised at Tess's appearance and tells her she believes neither Angel nor Tess could be at fault for whatever happened between them. Set to work digging and storing turnip roots, Marian and Tess get through the days by reminiscing about the time "they lived and loved together at Talbothays Dairy." Tess does not wear her wedding ring, does not wear the clothes he bought her, does not use his name, and will not tolerate Marian questioning her about Angel. As winter comes on, Izz Huett arrives to join her two friends. Tess falls behind doing the strenuous work of drawing reeds, and is harassed by her boss—who happens to be the Trantridge man who tried to insult her just before her marriage.

One day, Marian lets slip the story of Angel's invitation to Izz. This news makes Tess vow to address Clare; she starts but does not finish a letter to him. She does not believe she deserves any favor or pity from Angel or his family. In late December, though, she decides to visit Emminster to appeal to Angel's parents. She puts on her boots and walks 15 miles to the Clares' home. Ringing the doorbell, she gets no answer, and then, remembering they would be at church, she hides herself away to await their return. She places her boots to the side for safekeeping. While waiting, she overhears Angel's two brothers in conversation with Mercy Chant, criticizing Angel's unwise marriage. Mercy Chant spies Tess's boots and decides to take them to give to a poor person. Feeling scorned by the Clare family, Tess turns and walks back to Flintcomb-Ash. She does not realize that her husband's parents would have been far more sympathetic than his brothers.

Walking home, Tess spots a crowd listening to an itinerant preacher. The voice is familiar; startlingly, it sounds like that of her seducer, Alec. Rounding the corner, Tess studies the man, who truly is, she must soon believe, none other than Alec D'Urberville.

Analysis

Readers of the novel are, during this Phase, faced with the challenge of revising their opinion of Angel Clare, who turns from a potential savior of Tess into another one of her victimizers. Previously, his distinguished, caring, freethinking, and loving nature seemed to make him the ideal husband for Tess; now his limitations reveal themselves to a horrifying extent. It may be possible to feel something of Angel's misery at his discovery of Tess's affair, but it is impossible to avoid the word hypocritical in describing his application of the Victorian sexual double standard to their pasts. Tess has forgiven Angel his sin, but Angel absolutely cannot forgive Tess the same sin.

Hardy tells us that within Angel Clare's seemingly freethinking nature, there is "a hard logical deposit, like a vein of metal in soft loam, which turns the edge of everything that attempted to transverse it." No appeal, either to emotion or logic, will change Angel's mind once it is made up. His condemnation of Tess is marked by determination and not mere emotion. He willfully subdues the subtler emotion (love or protectiveness) to the grosser (jealousy and envy or hatred).

Tess's love for Angel, in great contrast, takes the form of an almost completely unquestioning loyalty. Her meekness allows Angel to determine their future: "her mood of long-suffering made his way easy for him." We can only assume Tess sees ultimate wisdom in Angel's coldness. We are reminded of her thoughts before her wedding. "Her one desire, so long resisted, to make herself his, to call him her lord, her own—then, if necessary, to die—had at last lifted her up…"

The final result of Tess's abandonment by Clare is her journey to Flintcomb-Ash. The portrait of the natural environment of this farm is a high point in Hardy's writing. The whole field was in color a desolate drab; it was a complexion without features, as if a face, from chin to brow, should be only an expanse of skin. The sky wore, in another color, the same likeness; a white vacuity of countenance with the lineaments gone. Across this field Tess and Marian crawl as if they were two flies. The descriptions of a drenching cold rain and of the onset of winter are finely detailed portraits which show Hardy's skill at communicating the reality of a brute physical nature. Again, Hardy shows an interaction between setting and mood.

Hardy broadens the book's struggle into a philosophical statement related to the Flintcomb-Ash environment, the cruelest and most desolate location in the story. Hardy notes that here, as everywhere, "two forces were at work..., the inherent will to enjoy, and the circumstantial will against enjoyment." Even in this most oppressive, inhuman environment, the world can be seen as composed of two opposing tendencies, and Hardy wishes us to note that the human will toward happiness is more powerful than the circumstances the world musters to defeat joy.

Hardy uses his persistent identification of Tess with Nature to delineate one of his principal themes, the opposition between Nature and society. Hardy assumes that society both creates and enforces guilt while Nature posits only the will to live and knows no moral distinctions. Once again, Tess is described as judging herself too harshly, by the limiting values of society rather than by the more vital impulses of Nature. "She was ashamed of herself for her gloom of the night, based on nothing more tangible than a sense of condemnation under an arbitrary law of society which has no foundation in Nature." Nothing Tess does contradicts Nature, but she continues to judge herself according to the artificial, arbitrary restrictions of civilization.

In a fashion typical of Victorian novels, Hardy crowds his canvas with a large variety of incidents. All events are more or less realistic, but some tend to the outlandish, and some are related more convincingly than others. Victorian audiences tended to be more accepting of coincidence and surprise than are contemporary readers. Many readers now find the sleepwalking scene in particular difficult to believe. However, there is no denying its dramatic boldness, and one can argue that Clare's expression of his unconscious thoughts is an effective way of showing his divided mind—which can accept his love for Tess only when its logical capacities are subdued. The scene in which Angel extends, than retracts, his offer

to Izz Huett is brilliantly constructed to evoke a strong pathos for the lovestruck but truthful Izz, who turns down a chance for happiness because she cannot lie about the purity of Tess's love for Angel. Other pathetic scenes adding to the near-melodramatic atmosphere of unrelieved misfortune include those of Tess articulating her lost hope for Angel's return and the sad, coincidence-laden misunderstanding when she visits the Clares' home in Emminster.

Phase the Fifth ends with a shock for which we have not been prepared, the discovery of Alec D'Urberville as a reformed man of the cloth. What this ironic change bodes for Tess is unfolded only in the next Phase of her life.

Study Questions

1. What prevents Angel from going into Tess's bedroom when he hears her breathing?

2. Why does Tess reject thoughts of suicide?

3. Where does Angel carry Tess in his sleep?

4. To what country does Angel decide to go?

5. What comment does her father make upon hearing that Tess has returned home?

6. Whom does Angel ask to accompany him overseas?

7. What are Tess's duties on the farm at Flintcomb-Ash?

8. What characters from Phase the First does Tess meet up with again at Flintcomb-Ash?

9. Who takes Tess's boots?

10. Whom does Tess observe preaching at a local barn?

Answers

1. The fearsome, sinister-looking portraits of the D'Urberville ancestors, which remind Angel of Tess, cause him to turn back.

2. She does not want her action to bring suspicion or discredit upon Angel.

3. He carries her over a footbridge and into an open coffin.

4. Angel decides to go to Brazil, to investigate farming opportunities.

5. He asks if she really got married this time, or if her present relationship with Angel is like her liaison with Alec.

6. Angel asks Izz Huett to go to Brazil and live with him, but soon comes to his senses and rescinds the impulsive offer.

7. Tess must dig up turnip roots so they can be eaten by livestock. Her other duties include trimming and storing those roots, as well as reed-drawing.

8. The Darch sisters, Car (the Queen of Spades) and Nancy (the Queen of Diamonds), are also working at Flintcomb-Ash.

9. Mercy Chant takes Tess's boots.

10. Tess spots Alec D'Urberville preaching to a crowd outside a barn as she walks back from Emminster to Flintcomb-Ash.

Suggested Essay Topics

1. Examine how the sexual double standard (the idea that men but not women are allowed sexual freedom) influences the characters and their actions in Phase the Fifth. Explain Hardy's title for this Phase: "The Woman Pays."

2. Analyze the metaphors which compare Tess to a trapped animal. How do these metaphors increase our sympathy for Tess? How do they further reinforce the connection between Tess and Nature?

3. Determine where this Phase fits on the pyramid of dramatic structure: antecedent action (what has taken place before the story proper starts), inciting moment (the catalyst which creates conflict and thus interest in the events to follow), rising action (the development of suspense and interest), climax (the most intense moment defining the protagonist's future), reversal (falling action, the playing out of previously established conflicts), or denouement (the tying up of loose ends). Defend your decision.

4. Analyze Angel's relationship with his parents. How do they both help and hinder Angel? What determines their behavior toward him? Why does Angel feel he must lie to them about the extent of his separation from Tess? Hardy indicts Angel for being a "slave to custom and conventionality": is this merely another way of stating the inevitable fact that he is the product of his particular upbringing?

5. In Chapter 40, Angel cries out, "O Tess! If you had only told me sooner, I would have forgiven you!" Is this the truth (making Tess again a victim of circumstances and bad timing), or is Hardy ironically showing us Angel attempting to deceive himself?

Phase the Sixth: The Convert
Chapters 45–52

New Character:

The man at the threshing machine: *a stranger to the agricultural world who operates a mechanical thresher, dictating an inhuman pace of work*

Summary

Tess can scarcely believe this man is Alec. His bold, masculine face is ill-adapted to the looks of a pious preacher. When he sees her, the effect is "electric." He is dumbstruck, briefly unable to preach. After finishing his sermon, Alec catches up to Tess. She wishes to have nothing to do with him; he claims merely to want to save her soul, on account of how he has "grievously wronged" her in the past. Tess scoffs at his conversion, which she thinks is an easy way for Alec to buy off the consequences of his evil deeds, and at his religious ideas, which she disbelieves because her husband has transmitted his own religious skepticism to her.

When they walk by a stone called "Cross-in-Hand" Alec asks Tess to swear that she will tempt him no longer. Tess reluctantly does so. The stone, she soon discovers, is not a holy relic as Alec said, but a "thing of ill omen" commemorating a murder.

Tess of the D'Urbervilles

A few days later, Alec finds Tess in the fields at Flintcomb-Ash. He wishes to inquire about her material condition. He offers a marriage license to Tess, who replies that she loves and is married to someone else. Alec realizes she is a deserted wife, and is upset that Tess will not allow him to protect her.

Later in February, Alec knocks at Tess's door, asking her to pray for him. "How can I pray for you," Tess asks, "when I am forbidden to believe that the great Power who moves the world would alter his plans on my account?" Tess says she has religion but doesn't believe in anything supernatural. She echoes to Alec several of the rationalist, anti-religious arguments she has learned from Angel Clare. These logical arguments demolish Alec's new-found religious convictions.

On a March morning, Tess is working at Flintcomb-Ash, feeding wheat into a mechanical thresher, when Alec, having shed his parson's outfit, seeks to talk to her. "You have been the cause of my backsliding," he says, "and you should be willing to share it, and leave that mule you call your husband for ever." Tess impulsively slaps him across the face, drawing blood. "Whip me, crush me," she baits him. "Once victim, always victim—that's the law!" He shakes her by the shoulders and tells her, "Remember, my lady, I was your master once! I will be your master again."

When Tess finishes the exhausting day's work, Alec reappears and walks her home. Going straight at Tess's chief anxiety, he informs Tess he has enough money to keep her family out of need. Tess hesitates before making a full refusal of this offer.

Once at her cottage, Tess writes a long, passionate letter to her husband, pleading for kind treatment. She is devoted to Angel but needs rescuing from an enemy.

Meanwhile, Angel, in Brazil, is reconsidering the entire moral scheme by which he has judged his wife. He realizes "the beauty or ugliness of a character lay not only in its achievements, but in its aims and impulses"—he should not blame Tess for what she did against her will. An Englishman who is his traveling companion advises Angel that he was wrong to leave Tess, that he should have judged her not according to what she had been in the past, but according to what she promised to be to him as a wife in the future. When this stranger dies of fever, Angel takes his words to heart and shifts from being Tess's critic to her advocate.

One morning, about a week before her term at Flintcomb-Ash is up, Tess's younger sister, 'Liza-Lu, arrives with dire family news. Joan is seriously ill and John, still in uncertain health, refuses to do any work. At home, Tess nurses her mother, who gets better, and works on the family garden so the family will have enough to eat.

One night, when she and other villagers are at work in a field burning brushes, Tess is surprised by the sight of Alec D'Urberville alongside her. Alluding both to the fires surrounding them and his persistent attempts to seduce the innocent Tess, Alec compares himself to Satan. Tess rejects the comparison. Alec again implores Tess to accept his help. She puts him off, though she knows how much her brothers and sisters could use D'Urberville's aid.

Walking home after this encounter, Tess is given startling news: her father has just died. His diseased heart finally gave way. The implications of his death go beyond the personal. The Durbeyfield family held the lease on their cottage only until John died. Thus, the family has to move, since the tenant-farmer wants the house for fieldworkers he wishes to hire. Although the family might be able to stay on as weekly tenants, the shiftlessness of the family, the queerness of the unions made by Tess, and the undesirable social independence of families of this artisanal class, lead to the Durbeyfields being put out. It is doubtful that their ancestors gave such rude treatment to others in the time of their ascendancy.

Joan decides the family will seek lodgings at Kingsbere, the town in which lies the cathedral containing the D'Urberville family vaults. On Old Lady-Day, the day when many country laborers choose or are forced to find new jobs and residences, the Durbeyfields pack up their belongings and leave Marlott. When they get to Kingsbere, they discover their letter asking for rooms has arrived too late. There is no shelter for them. On a whim, Joan unpacks a bed underneath the church wall, directly below a stained-glass window named after the D'Urbervilles.

Alec rides up and tells Tess of the legend of the D'Urberville coach: those of D'Urberville blood are prone to hear the sound of a non-existent coach. The story dates back to an abduction and murder involving a D'Urberville. Alec offers to allow them to live at Trantridge; Joan can have a job tending fowl. Tess is barely able to refuse this necessary help. Seeking solace amid the vaults, or graves, of her ancestors in the Kingsbere cathedral, she is taken aback by the sight of D'Urberville reclining on one of the tombs. He can do more for her than can any of the real D'Urbervilles lying in these vaults, he boasts. Looking at the entrance to the vaults, Tess wonders, "Why am I on the wrong side of this door!"

Meanwhile, Marian and Izz decide they must take action to repair the marriage of their friends. They write a brief, plain letter to Angel at Emminster warning him to look after his wife because she is being set upon by an enemy.

Analysis

Phase the Sixth is the most eventful of the novel. Material is presented that relates to every theme in the book. All three principal characters, and the changes they undergo, influence the story, while the narrative also incorporates major segments of the lives of secondary characters such as Tess's family. The issues of religion and morality are presented through the stories of Alec's religious conversion, his conflict and arguments with Tess, and the changes Angel undergoes in Brazil. The final decline of Tess's family and the mechanized nature of the farmwork at Flintcomb-Ash provide Hardy an opportunity to introduce the social and economic shifts that influence her downfall.

Tess herself undergoes a major psychological change in this Phase, being so worked over by circumstances that she yields to D'Urberville a second time, again contrary to her moral nature and better judgment. The pattern of her harassment by forces outside herself, including individuals such as D'Urberville and the absent Clare, as well as more impersonal forces, such as a changing economic order, her position at the tail end of the decayed D'Urberville family, and the implacable ironies of life itself, continues like a drumbeat throughout Phase the Sixth. Although Hardy does not announce it in so many words, Tess makes the decision at the end of this Phase to trade her body to D'Urberville for his support of her family. It is a decision that ultimately seals her fate. The psychological stress prior to this decision can be measured by the differences between her two letters to Clare. The first, longer one admits that she deserves punishment but pleads for the husband she loves greatly to treat her kindly. The second letter is an expression of anger and outrage at the injustice she has been dealt by Angel. For the first time, Tess realizes that she is not at fault and that the punishment she has received has been unfair. She has committed sins of inadvertence, not of intention.

The first few chapters expose Tess to an Alec D'Urberville outwardly quite different from the one we remember. These changes allow Hardy to introduce an important and topical debate about religion and morality into his novel. Later, after the religious conversion does not "take," Hardy emphasizes Alec's relentless physical pursuit of Tess. Wherever Tess goes, Alec finds her. He even adopts a comic disguise when he wears an old-fashioned rural smockfrock to surprise Tess when she is living at Marlott. However Alec dresses or disguises himself, he is dangerous to Tess.

Further evidence of Tess's moral purity in the face of continual poverty, stress, and temptation comes, in fact, from an unlikely source, the mouth of Alec D'Urberville. Alec sees Tess as guiltless in their affair and as the only innocent woman he has ever known. He says she is "unsmirched in spite of all." At some moments, he rather convincingly plays the part of a rejected lover seeking a renewed relationship, as when he forlornly rips up the marriage license Tess has declined.

Alec experiences numerous changes of personality in this Phase. The first one, his conversion to the extreme Calvinism of Reverend Clare, is one for which we have not been prepared. The sight of Alec preaching the word of God is just as strange to us as it is to Tess. Hardy depicts Alec in such a manner that we can easily share Tess's idea that there is something fraudulent and cynical about his religious conversion. Alec compares the spiritual satisfaction of his religion to the masochistic "pleasure of having a good slap at yourself"; his conversion, he says, came upon him as a "jolly good idea." Alec's unseriousness and villainy serve to emphasize the singular goodness of the pure Tess.

The religious arguments between Alec and Tess substantiate a theme of concern to Hardy and other Victorians, which is the relationship of religion to morality. Tess becomes the spokesperson for Hardy's own sense of religious skepticism. Hardy does not choose to write out fully the anti-religious beliefs shared by Angel and Tess. In this choice, we can measure the distance between Hardy's novel and the traditional novel of ideas, in which characters give long speeches explaining and defending their opinions and beliefs. We know that Tess is Hardy's heroine and Alec is the villain, and we perceive that Alec's Calvinist-flavored dogma is being suggested as the "wrong" alternative to Tess's correct religion of "loving-kindness," a version of Christianity stripped of supernaturalism down to its supposed essence in the Sermon on the Mount (Christ's lesson on the importance of mercy and compassion).

A major issue in Victorian thought concerned the maintenance of ethics in the absence of an agreed-upon religion. If religion were to be discredited, how could people be trusted to act morally and ethically, and if people could not be so trusted, how could society remain cohesive? Religious freethinkers claimed that individual humans could, and would have to be, trusted as the guardians and enforcers of their own moral authenticity. The traditionalist's counterargument relied upon reasoning similar to Alec's statement: "If there's nobody to say, 'Do this, and it will be a good thing for you after you are dead; do that, and it will be a bad thing for you,' I can't warm up...I am not going to feel responsible for my deeds and passions if there's nobody to be responsible to." But Alec, as we see repeatedly, is just the sort of person incapable of resisting the urge to harm others. Lacking the innate "loving-kindness" Tess espouses, Alec needs to imagine a "boss" outside himself who will punish him when he is bad and reward him when he is good. In contrast to Tess, he cannot be responsible for himself.

Hardy develops a further aspect of the question of moral behavior and judgment through the changes undergone by Angel in this Phase. Angel surmounts his own previous doubts about Tess as he learns a new, more charitable, less orthodox definition of morality. "Having long discredited the old systems of mysticism, he now began to discredit the old appraisements of morality. He thought they wanted readjusting. Who was the moral man? Still more pertinently, who was the moral woman? The beauty or ugliness of a character lay not only in its achievements, but in its aims and impulses; its true history lay, not only among things done, but among things willed." Morality is not a simple, legalistic equation of particular deeds with particular sins. In judging, what must be taken into account is what the person wanted and willed, not just what they did or were influenced, or perhaps forced, to do. In sum, what one does is not equal to what one is. If we judge only by what someone did, we will ignore the quality of their hearts and minds, their truest moral tendencies. Angel learns that anyone who wishes to be a moral judge of others incurs a deep responsibility to perceive correctly.

The steam-driven threshing machine is described so vividly by Hardy that we can imagine it to be another of the characters victimizing Tess. The mechanical thresher, that red tyrant, is a representative of the modern, industrialized world which is destroying the traditional independence and human rhythms of the agricultural community. The thresher, operated by an engineer from the north of England, makes despotic demands upon the endurance of those who must work on it. It produces, in short, alienated labor. In Tess's case, she is again victimized in being denied control by the thresher over her body. Hardy conjoins the thresher scene, representing economic oppression, with another visit from Alec, representing sexual oppression.

As Phase the Sixth moves towards completion, Hardy puts all the necessary plot machinery in place to drive the novel towards its ultimate conclusion. Different characters are (even if unwittingly) working for and against Tess as if engaged in a battle to claim her. The stranger who befriends Angel in Brazil gives Clare a new philosophy and a new outlook on Tess. Izz Huett and Marian try, through their letter, to reunite Angel with Tess. Alec and the thresher attempt to keep Tess away from Angel, and deprived of any capacity for independence. These forces arrayed for and against Tess take on the aspect of good versus evil. Izz, Marian, and Clare's friend are positive, moral, sympathetic forces. The thresher and Alec are described as negative, diabolic, and oppressive.

Phase the Sixth contains Hardy's most important and sustained association of Tess's downfall with her socioeconomic position. Hardy's focus is on the individual tragedy of Tess, but he continually returns to the theme of the tragic destruction of the traditional English rural village, most directly in the following passage describing the Durbeyfields being put out: "The village had formerly contained, side by side with the agricultural laborers, an interesting and better-informed class, ranking distinctly above the former—

the class to which Tess's father and mother had belonged…: a set of people who owed a certain stability of aim and conduct to the fact of their being lifeholders like Tess's father, or copyholders, or, occasionally, small freeholders. But as the long holdings fell in they were seldom let again to similar tenants, and were mostly pulled down, if not absolutely required by the farmer for his hands. Cottagers who were not directly employed on the land were looked down upon with disfavour, and the banishment of some starved the trade of others…These families, who had formed the backbone of village life in the past, who were the depositaries of the village traditions, had to seek refuge in the large centres; the process humorously designated by the statisticians as the tendency of the rural populations toward the large towns, being really the tendency of water to flow uphill when forced by machinery."

Hardy thus includes the tragedy of Tess and the destruction of her family within the larger socioeconomic contexts of the agricultural unrest and the depopulation of the countryside. From this point of view, Tess's sufferings seem not arbitrary or unique but rather become part of the decline of her class. The villain of this piece, we see from Hardy's conclusion here, is machinery. The forces of mechanization make their most significant appearance in the novel in the form of the recently described threshing machine. We can also note that Hardy's family came from the rural class of the Durbeyfields—slightly above the farm laborers, but never far enough above that class to experience complete economic stability.

Study Questions

1. Does Tess believe Alec's conversion?

2. With what does Tess strike Alec?

3. What happens when the rick (or pile) of wheat is nearly levelled?

4. What advice does Angel receive from the cosmopolitan Englishman he meets in Brazil?

5. What are the implications of John's death?

6. To what figure does Alec compare himself when he surprises Tess in a field?

7.   What is the story of the D'Urberville Coach?

8.   What generally happens each Old Lady-Day?

9.   Where do Tess and her family decide to make a new home?

10.   What advice do Izz and Marian give Angel?

Answers

1.   Tess cannot believe that Alec has truly been converted.

2.   Tess hits Alec across the face with her rough leather gloves.

3.   The rats which have taken refuge near the bottom of the rick must be caught. This activity sometimes draws a crowd of observers from the area.

4.   Angel is told that he was foolish in rejecting a woman who loves him, and wrong in estimating what Tess would be as a wife solely by what she had been in the past.

5.   The Durbeyfield family had the lease on their cottage only until John died. Thus, the family has to move, since the owner wants the house for fieldworkers he wishes to hire.

6.   Alec compares himself to Satan, the Eternal Tempter. Surprisingly enough, Tess rejects this comparison.

7.   The legend of the coach is that those of D'Urberville blood are prone to hear the sound of a non-existent coach. The legend dates back to an abduction and murder involving a D'Urberville.

8.   Laborers and artisans frequently start new jobs in different towns, areas, or farms, and are forced to move.

9.   Tess and her family move to Kingsbere, the town in which lies the cathedral containing the D'Urberville family vaults (graves).

10.   Izz and Marian urge Angel to take care of his wife because she is being set upon by an enemy.

Suggested Essay Topics

1.   Alec D'Urberville shows new aspects to his character in Phase the Sixth. Analyze how we judge Alec less harshly after

this Phase—how does he show himself to be a better, more considerate, less purely villainous person than we might have believed him to be earlier? Are his actions toward Tess ever motivated by love?

2. "And yet these harshnesses [of individual men to individual women and vice versa] are tenderness itself when compared with the universal harshness out of which they grow; the harshness of the position towards the temperament, of the means towards the aims, of to-day towards yesterday, of here-after towards to-day." Define these "harshnesses" in your own words, and then try to account for the presence of this sentence in the novel. Does Hardy detract from his novel by inserting such philosophical generalities? Or do they make profound sense against the background of the novel's plot?

3. How do larger economic and demographic forces affect the social class occupied by the Durbeyfield family?

4. A protagonist is defined as "the leading character or principal figure in a narrative." The form and sequence of a novel arise from the delineation of the growth and complexity of a protagonist. Demonstrate that this Phase has two protagonists, Tess and Angel.

Phase the Seventh: Fulfillment
Chapters 53–59

New Characters:

A family of farm laborers: *the new inhabitants of the cottage where the Durbeyfields once lived*

Mrs. Brooks: *a generally uncurious landlady at a fashionable Sandbourne lodging-house*

A Sandbourne workman: *the first to view D'Urberville's corpse*

The caretaker at Bramshurst Court: *a woman who oversees a property for its owners*

Sixteen policemen: *hunters of a wanted murderess*

Summary

Angel Clare returns home to Emminster so ravaged by his illness that his parents can scarcely recognize him. When his mother wonders why Angel is so anxious about a "mere child of the soil," Angel reveals that Tess is a member of the ancient D'Urberville family.

Angel sends a letter to Marlott looking for Tess. A reply comes from Joan, who informs him that Tess is gone from her, but that she will write Angel when she returns. Angel is chastened by his treatment of Tess. He wonders why he did not view his wife "constructively rather than biographically, by the will rather than by the deed." His father tells him Tess never asked the Clares for any money during his sojourn, and Angel begins to realize how much Tess has suffered.

Angel goes to Flintcomb-Ash in search of Tess and then on to Marlott. He learns Tess has not used her married name in his absence. In Marlott, he discovers Tess and her family are no longer living at their cottage, which is now inhabited by a family concerned only with its own circumstances and completely ignorant of Tess's history. Angel sees the elaborately carved headstone of John, which details his illustrious ancestry. When he discovers the carver has not been paid, he does a good turn for the Durbeyfields by paying off the bill.

Angel is able to find Joan at Kingsbere. Their meeting is awkward, but Joan tells him Tess is at Sandbourne, a local resort town, at an address unknown to Joan.

Angel Clare arrives in Sandbourne the next day. Asking around for a Mrs. Clare or a Miss Durbeyfield, Angel receives no information. A local postman says there is a Mrs. D'Urberville at a lodging house called The Herons. When Angel announces himself to the landlady, Tess herself descends the stairs.

It is a much-changed Tess: she is dressed in luxurious clothes, evidently given her by D'Urberville. Angel pleads for forgiveness. He now appreciates Tess for what she is. "Too late, too late!" cries Tess in response; D'Urberville has won her back; she no longer cares what happens to her. The unhappy pair stand paralyzed, seeming to "implore something to shelter them from reality."

The landlady of The Herons, Mrs. Brooks, is a usually incurious woman, but Angel's visit leads her to eavesdrop at the keyhole

of Tess and Alec's room. She hears Tess remonstrating Alec for caus-
ing her to lose Angel a second time, and she hears Alec's sharp reply. A little while later, she notices what seems to be a bloodstain
on the ceiling above her. She flags down a local workman, who goes
into the D'Urberville suite and discovers that Alec D'Urberville has
been stabbed to death.

Meanwhile, Angel has gone to the train station. Running towards him, he sees, is a woman—Tess, who wishes to tell her husband that she has killed D'Urberville. Though he scarcely believes
this news, Angel is at last completely tender toward his wife. He
must now be her protector. The pair walk northward on remote
footpaths. When they see a mansion called Bramshurst Court,
unoccupied because it is for rent, they decide to take refuge there.

By unspoken consent, Angel and Tess do not speak of anything
that happened after their marriage. They spend five days of bliss
isolated from the world, experiencing "affection, union, error forgiven," until the caretaker notices their presence. Tess does not
want to, but they leave, planning an escape from England out of a
northern port town.

That night, they stumble across a series of stone pillars which
make an odd humming sound in the wind. Angel realizes the place
is Stonehenge, the ancient temple at which heathens made sacri-
fices to the sun. Tess lays herself down upon an altar stone. Tess
asks Angel to marry her younger sister 'Liza-Lu, who has all the
good qualities of Tess and none of the bad, when she herself is
gone. Angel is shocked at the idea.

In the light of dawn, Angel sees a group of men advancing toward the ancient monument. He implores the men to leave Tess
alone until she wakes. When Tess rises, she accepts her capture: "It
is as it should be...I am ready."

The scene shifts to Wintoncester, once capital of Wessex.
The view of this city is dominated by an ugly, red-brick jail. Standing on a nearby hillside just outside of town, Angel and 'Liza-Lu
hold hands as they see a black flag rise up over the jail. Tess
Durbeyfield has been executed. "'Justice' was done, and the President of the Immortals, in Aeschylean phrase, had ended his sport
with Tess."

Analysis

The title of the novel's final Phase, "Fulfillment," is ironic but accurate. Tess, the ultimate victim, can find peace, happiness, and content only outside this world, not in it. Her victimization—by Fate, by historical conditions, by her family, by social standards, by D'Urberville, by Clare—is so complete that it seems as if Tess is being hounded from this world.

In their temporary hideaway at Bramshurst Court, hidden from the sight of the world, Tess and Angel experience a brief period of contentment. Only away from the moral codes of the world can Angel and Tess experience the happiness they deserve, a state of "affection, union, error forgiven."

Hardy's use of Stonehenge as a setting allows him a final echo of several important patterns of reference. The motif of Tess being hunted and pursued is underscored visually by the scene in which Tess awakes at dawn surrounded by a circle of policemen, official guardians of the social morality Tess has continually been punished by. Her connection to Nature and to paganism makes this ancient monument an appropriate setting. Tess herself notes Angel used to call her a heathen. The connection between Tess and places of death reaches a culmination here. Tess finds final rest on an altar, or place of sacrifice. The sense of present action being only part of a vast history—Hardy's appeal to an ultra-historic imagination— is activated through the use of this ancient historical site.

Tess's tragic victimization points to a new set of possibilities for human conduct. Her devotion to Clare establishes a new vision of selfless love. She is so forward-looking and selfless that she urges Angel to marry 'Liza-Lu, whom Tess thinks is a better, and Hardy calls a more spiritualized, version of herself. Tess becomes not the illustration of a thesis (about the decline of the peasantry or the sexual double standard) but, as in the stories of saint's lives, a person who lived an exceptional life.

In tragic fashion, Tess comes to experience a new orientation to the world, completely different from the everyday way we typically view life. She experiences her pain not as material fact but as a sort of transcendence. Tess welcomes the final punishments of capture and execution. Of what does Tess speak when she greets the policemen who will arrest her with the phrase, "I am ready"?

On the Darwinian level, we might say the final rhythm of the life of a species, extinction, has been reached. Tess was born, reproduced, tried to adapt to a cruel world, and now will die. On a tragic level, we might say Tess's assent to her victimization is a final, ennobling act of forgiveness toward the world.

Hardy underscores the tragic atmosphere by a series of references to famous tragedies of Western literature. Stonehenge, the monument to the sun, recalls the sun-blasted heath upon which Lear, in Shakespeare's *King Lear*, experiences his re-evaluation of life. Tess's "I am ready" echoes Edgar's death-embracing statement "Readiness is all" from the same play. The last image of the book, Angel and 'Liza-Lu walking hand-in-hand, recalls the final moment of John Milton's epic *Paradise Lost*, in which Adam and Eve move hand-in-hand into a fallen world in which they must exercise choice and moral responsibility.

Most famously, Hardy refers to the Greek tragedian Aeschylus to describe the malignant plan the universe had in store for Tess Durbeyfield: "'Justice' was done, and the President of the Immortals, in Aeschylean phrase, has ended his sport with Tess." This bitter statement encapsulates the idea that some higher power has victimized Tess, and has probably done so just for fun. Whatever term we use for the Supreme Being, this figure does not have the best interests of humans at heart. Although this categorical skepticism may not be all that surprising contemporarily, the majority of the novel's detractors passionately disapproved of these lines' belief that the universe is not controlled by a beneficent, Christian God.

Our final impression of the novel does not have to do with a philosophical lesson on the existence of God, or an illustration of historic and economic forces. What we are left with is a feeling of profound, humanistic sympathy for Tess Durbeyfield, pure woman and pure victim.

Study Questions

1. How is Angel Clare's health after his journey to Brazil?

2. What causes Angel Clare finally to reveal Tess's noble blood?

3. What does Angel discover when he reaches Tess's Marlott cottage?

4. Where does Joan tell Angel to seek Tess?

5. What does Tess say when Angel asks forgiveness for leaving her?

6. How is the death of D'Urberville discovered?

7. What does the bloodstain seem to resemble?

8. What is the location of the lovers' temporary refuge from the law?

9. At what monument is Tess taken prisoner?

10. What two characters see a sign of Tess's execution?

Answers

1. Angel is weak and emaciated after living through an attack of fever in Brazil.

2. After Mrs. Clare refers to Angel's wife as a "mere child of the soil," Angel tells his parents of Tess's ancestry.

3. Angel discovers the Durbeyfields have been turned out of the cottage and that a new family is living there.

4. Joan tells Angel that Tess is living at Sandbourne, a fashionable seaside resort. Joan does not know the exact address.

5. Tess cries "Too late"—she has been won back by D'Urberville.

6. Mrs. Brooks, the landlady, notices a bloodstain and gets a local workman to go inside the room to see what has happened.

7. Alec's blood, after leaving his body, takes shape as a large ace of hearts.

8. Angel and Tess take shelter at a mansion called Bramshurst Court that is being offered for rent.

9. Tess is captured at Stonehenge.

10. Angel and 'Liza-Lu see a black flag, the sign of Tess's execution.

Suggested Essay Topics

1. Phase the Seventh acquires an aura of inevitability because its events are so heavily influenced by the past. The past is a recurrent force which determines what happens in the present. Write about the connections between past events and the incidents of Phase the Seventh. Analyze the many parallels and repetitions Hardy inserts in the conclusion of his book. For example: Angel meets Tess at a lodging house called The Heron, while their courting went on in early morning surrounded by herons (Phase the Third); Angel asks Tess, unsuccessfully, for forgiveness, just as Tess did of Angel; Angel's casual remark in Phase the Fifth about Alec being still alive has apparently stayed in Tess's mind and compelled her to kill Alec. Does Hardy persuade us of the idea that the past cannot be escaped? How do these connections lend unity to the novel?

2. Analyze the levels of symbolism and patterns of reference that culminate in the Stonehenge scene.

3. Explain the significance of the final lines: " 'Justice' was done, and the President of the Immortals, in Aeschylean phrase, had ended his sport with Tess. And the D'Urberville knights and dames slept on in their tombs unknowing." Points to explain would include the meaning of the quotation marks around "Justice," the interpretation of the phrase "President of the Immortals," and the significance of the book's final reference to the extinct and useless D'Urberville nobility. You may also compare this line to Hardy's 1891 version, which substitutes "Time, the Arch-satirist" for "President of the Immortals."

Sample Analytical Paper Topics

The following paper topics are based on the entire book. Following each topic is a thesis and sample outline. Use these as a starting point for your paper. Each major point in your essay should refer to at least one quote from the novel, properly introduced and explained.

Topic #1

Hardy defines tragedy as "the worthy encompassed by the inevitable" and adds that the tragedies of immoral and worthless people are not of the best. Interpret *Tess of the D'Urbervilles* as a tragedy, using these ideas.

Outline

I.   Thesis Statement: Tess of the D'Urbervilles *is a tragedy because it depicts the destruction of a morally worthy person by inevitable and unalterable forces outside human control.*

II. Tess Durbeyfield is continually depicted as innocent, conscientious, and morally pure

    A. The novelist repeatedly uses words such as innocent and pure to describe Tess

    B. Her thoughts are always to help her family, not herself

    C. She is a creature of Nature

    D. Tess is a morally pure woman, despite her actions

1. Hardy's subtitle shows his evaluation of her

2. Both Angel and Alec accept Tess as pure

3. Tess's actions of submitting to Alec and later killing him are motivated only by need and desperation

4. Tess shows more moral understanding than anyone else in the novel

III. Tess is brought down by a variety of forces which neither she nor anyone else would have been able to stop

   A. Tess is victimized by people more powerful than she

   B. The world is malignantly organized to deny human happiness

   C. Historical and social forces render Tess vulnerable to exploitation

IV. Tess's downfall is partially caused by what she cannot help, her ancestry as a D'Urberville

   A. She has inherited a slight incautiousness of character from her family

   B. She is being paid back for all the ways the ancient D'Urbervilles victimized others when they were powerful

   C. The decline of the D'Urberville family is irreversible

V. Hardy depicts Tess's downfall as one in a series of tragedies representative of human history

   A. As Tess says, her life is just like that of thousands before and after her

   B. References to classical and Shakespearean tragedy show Tess as related to other tragic victims

Topic #2

Analyze the role of religion and religious faith in the book. How are the characters motivated by their religious beliefs or doubts? What does Hardy wish to say about the practice of religion?

Outline

I.   Thesis Statement: *Thomas Hardy depicts the characters of* Tess of the D'Urbervilles *to suggest that moral purity is not necessarily related to religious orthodoxy.*

II. The two most important and morally worthy characters experience religious doubts

    A.   Tess admits she does not know the Lord yet

        1.   She cannot accept that God would want her to feel so sinful

    B.   Angel goes through the religious doubts of his age

III. The best thing about Angel's parents is their charity, not their Calvinist earnestness

    A.   Reverend Clare is warm-hearted

    B.   Mrs. Clare is able to sympathize with her son

IV. Tess's moral purity is not related to her churchgoing

    A.   Tess is pure and innocent because of her innate nature and the strength of her conscience

V.   Hardy presents several characters associated with religion in a harsh, satiric light

    A.   The parson is a man of little charity

    B.   Mercy Chant inadvertently becomes another victimizer of Tess

    C.   Reverend Cuthbert and Felix Clare are limited people

    D.   Alec's conversion shows that even the sinful can appear to be religious

Topic #3

Show how Hardy's descriptions of landscapes and the environment convey his idea of the centrality of Nature to human life.

Outline

I.   Thesis Statement: *To Thomas Hardy, Nature is an ever-present aspect of life.*

II.   The happenings at Talbothays are an outgrowth of the fertile natural environment

    A.   Descriptions of weather and growth are linked to Tess's courtship

III. Every Phase of the novel contains references to natural landscapes and natural facts

    A.   Phase the Second contains a scene of reaping wheat

    B.   Tess must walk 15 cold and muddy miles back from Emminster to Flintcomb-Ash without her boots

    C.   Flintcomb-Ash is desolate and barren

IV.   Tess is a field woman, pure and simple

    A.   She is most happy when doing outdoor work

V.   Hardy's metaphors frequently rely on natural elements

    A.   When Tess is upset, the sky looks like a wound

    B.   Tess's situation is paralleled to that of dying pheasants

Topic #4

The one key factor in Tess's downfall is her gender. Her tragedy is a woman's tragedy.

Outline

I.   Thesis Statement: *Tess's tragedy is a direct result of the lack of social and personal opportunities afforded to women in a male-dominated country.*

II.   She has internalized the lack of self-esteem forced upon women

    A.   She speaks of wishing to die

    B.   She speaks of the shame of ever having been born

    C.   She is excessively deferential to Clare. She wishes to think of him as her lord and master and even to die for him

    D.   She internally accepts that she is guilty for having committed the same action as did Clare

III. Tess is continually victimized by men who assume they have the right to control or judge her

    A. The powerful Alec is able to have his way with her

    B. Angel punishes her because he fails to see the reality of who Tess is

    C. Minor characters such as the parson and Farmer Groby harass Tess

IV. As a poor peasant woman, Tess has few opportunities to make a living and explore the world

    A. Her lack of education cuts off her knowledge of other opportunities in the world

    B. She must implore men like Alec and Angel to be her protector

    C. Her family exploits her to help out their finances

Bibliography

Butler, Lance St. John. *Thomas Hardy*. Cambridge: Cambridge University Press, 1978.

Gittings, Robert. *Young Thomas Hardy*. London: Heinemann, 1975.

Gregor, Ian. *The Great Web*. London: Faber, 1974.

Guerard, A. J. (ed.). *Hardy: A Collection of Critical Essays*. Englewood Cliffs, NJ: Prentice-Hall, 1963.

Hardy, F. E. *The Life of Thomas Hardy*. London: Macmillan, 1962.

Hardy, Thomas. *Tess of the D'Urbervilles*. Edited and with introduction by William E. Buckler. Riverside Editions. New York: Houghton Mifflin Company, 1960.